THE
AUTOBIOGRAPHY
OF AN
EXECUTION

THE AUTOBIOGRAPHY OF AN EXECUTION

DAVID R. DOW

TWELVE

NEW YORK   BOSTON

Twelve
Hachette Book Group
237 Park Avenue
New York, NY 10017

www.HachetteBookGroup.com

Twelve is an imprint of Grand Central Publishing.
The Twelve name and logo are trademarks of Hachette Book Group, Inc.

Printed in the United States of America

First Edition: February 2010
10 9 8 7 6 5 4 3 2 1

Library of Congress Cataloging-in-Publication Data

Dow, David R.
  The autobiography of an execution / David R. Dow.—1st ed.
    p. cm.
  Summary: "A riveting, artfully written memoir of a lawyer's life as he races to prevent death row inmates from being executed"—Provided by the publisher.
  ISBN 978-0-446-56206-5
  1. Dow, David R. 2. Law teachers—Texas—Houston—Biography. 3. Capital punishment—Texas. I. Title.
  KF373.D635A3 2010
  345.764'0773—dc22
  [B]   2009023424

In Memory of Peter G.

Qué significa persistir
en el callejón de la muerte?

PABLO NERUDA,
El libro de las preguntas, LXII

He thought that in the history of the world it might even be
that there was more punishment than crime but he took small
comfort from it.

CORMAC MCCARTHY, *The Road*

AUTHOR'S NOTE

I have been representing death-row inmates, mostly in Texas, since the late 1980s. The stories in this book are true. I was involved in all the cases I have described (although not always as the lead lawyer), and all the factual details are based on my own firsthand knowledge. I have not exaggerated to heighten drama.

In telling these stories, however, I have confronted constraints. A lawyer's obligation to keep his client's secrets confidential remains even after the client has died. I have therefore changed many of the names, and I have altered many identifying details.

In addition to using pseudonyms, I have occasionally changed genders, ages, races, locations (including cities), dates, and restaurants. I have not altered the facts of the crimes nor of my relationships with my clients, but I have taken procedural details of some cases and attributed them to other cases. In some cases where there were multiple execution dates, I have told the story as if there was only one. I have transposed the geographical location of certain events (including where certain things took place inside the prison or jail, which county some crimes were committed in, and whether a legal proceeding took place in state or federal court), and I've altered the timing of others, though the basic chronology of events is accurate.

I have also probably put some of Katya's words in my mouth, and vice versa. I recall many of our conversations with near-perfect clarity (although, as she will tell you, I forget many more), but I often recall what was said without remembering which one of us said it.

Scores of lawyers have worked on the cases I describe in the following pages. To avoid burdening the reader with a Shakespearean cast, I refer to only three of them, using pseudonyms, in the text. I list all their actual names in the Acknowledgments.

I have made the changes I did for many reasons: to protect attorney-client privilege, as I said, which survives even after the client dies; to avoid revealing confidential information of present and former clients; to protect the families of both murder victims and the criminals who killed them (even families of murderers are entitled to privacy and respect); to conceal the identities of people who would not want their help to me revealed (including guards, police officers, court personnel, judges, and prosecutors); to protect living clients from retaliation or jealousy; to compress into a two- or three-year period stories that in some cases lasted a decade or longer; and to tell the stories without getting too bogged down in legal and procedural details. I have endeavored to write an honest memoir without revealing confidences, so I have told these stories in a way that is faithful to the truth as well as to the individuals they feature.

THE
AUTOBIOGRAPHY
OF AN
EXECUTION

If you knew at precisely what time on exactly what day you were going to die, and that date arrived, and the hour and minute came and went, and you were not dead, would you be able to enjoy each additional second of your life, or would you be filled with dreadful anticipation that would turn relief into torture? That is the question I asked myself at twenty minutes past eight o'clock on Halloween night. Jeremy Winston was still alive. He was in the holding cell, eight steps away from the execution chamber at the Walls Unit in Huntsville, Texas. He was supposed to have been dead for two hours.

Winston was my client. I was sitting in my office in Houston with three other lawyers, waiting for the clerk's office at the United States Supreme Court to call. The warden at the Walls was holding a judicial order instructing him to execute Winston after 6:00 p.m. He would carry it out unless the Supreme Court intervened. Winston had been pacing for two hours in the tiny holding cell, three steps one way, three steps back. He had requested a cigarette in lieu of a final meal. Prison officials informed him that tobacco products were not permitted on prison grounds. But the three guards who would escort

1

Winston to the gurney gave him a pack of cigarettes and one match. He lit each new cigarette with the dregs of the old one.

Our phone rang. The clerk at the Supreme Court wanted to know what time we would be filing additional papers. I hadn't planned to file anything else. The four of us working on the case had already written our best argument and sent it to the Court. It had been there since five o'clock. In nearly twenty years of representing death-row inmates, this had never happened to me before. Was the clerk telling us to file something? I told him I'd call right back.

Had a law clerk or even a Supreme Court justice seen some argument that we had missed and decided to hold the case a little bit longer, giving us more time for the lightbulb to click on? That's what the justices do sometimes, they toy with you. Jerome, Gary, Kassie, and I were sitting in the conference room. We frantically deconstructed and reassembled our arguments, looking for something we might have missed. I was bouncing a Super Ball off the wall, tossing it with my left hand and catching the rebound with my right. Gary was juggling three beanbags. Jerome and Kassie were sitting still, pens in their hands, waiting to write something down, if we could think of something to write. Jeremy Winston was wondering why he was still alive. Suddenly I saw him, peering into the conference room, watching his lawyers juggle and play catch and sit there doing nothing. He shook his head, a gesture just short of disgust, realizing the sand was about to run out.

Maybe, I said, we had called something by the wrong name. You might think that when a life is at stake, formal legal rules would not matter so much, but you would be wrong. People die when their lawyers neglect to dot the *i*'s or cross the *t*'s. I decided we

2

would refile what we had already filed, and just call it something different. Because I couldn't think of any other explanation, I convinced myself the problem was with the title. Necessity's eldest child is invention; her second-born is rationalization. Gary's the fastest typist. I asked him to get started working on it.

Two minutes later the phone rang again. Kassie answered. The clerk was calling to tell us never mind, that we had lost. I went into my office, closed the door, and called Winston to let him know. He was declared dead at twenty-seven minutes past nine.

■ ■ ■

I WALKED IN THE DOOR from the garage at nine fifty-five. I was sucking on a peppermint to hide that I had been smoking. A dried-out roasted chicken was sitting on the counter. A fly was on the drumstick. I shooed it away. An open bottle of red wine was next to the chicken. I called to my wife, Katya. There was no answer. I figured Lincoln had had a nightmare and she was upstairs with him. I started to climb the stairs. Katya called to me from the library. She was sitting on the sofa, her feet on the coffee table, holding a wineglass on her stomach. Her eyes were red. She had been crying.

What's the matter? I said.

Where were you?

At my office. The Supreme Court didn't call until after eight. Winston didn't get executed until after nine. What's the matter?

You were supposed to take Lincoln to the haunted house. He waited up until nearly eight.

Oh shit. I completely forgot.

Lincoln was six. I had expected to be home by 7:00 at the latest. I told him I would take him to the haunted house after he collected enough candy. He had made me a costume to wear. I said, Why didn't you call to remind me?

I did call you. I left three messages on your cell phone.

I told her I had left my cell phone in my car. I asked, Why didn't you call the office?

Because I didn't think you would still be there. You always call when something happens. The execution was supposed to be at six, right?

Yes, it was supposed to be, I said. Did you go without me?

No. He said he wanted to wait for you. I told him I didn't know when you were going to be home. He said that he would just wait. He kept his Thomas the Tank Engine outfit on and sat on the stairs. At seven thirty I told him the haunted house was going to close in a few minutes, but he said he'd keep waiting. He came and sat outside with Winona and me to hand out candy to the trick-or-treaters. At eight I told him it was time to go to bed. On the way upstairs he said that he was feeling a little sad. I told him that it was okay to be sad. I said that you had probably gotten busy at work. He said, I know, but I'm still disappointed.

I said, Crap. I can't believe I forgot this. I'm going upstairs to check on him. I'll be right down.

I peeked in his room. Winona, our seventy-five-pound red Doberman, was lying on the bed, her head resting on Lincoln's ankles. He said, Hi, Dada. You missed the haunted house.

I said, I know I did, amigo. I'm really sorry. I forgot all about it. Can you forgive me?

He said, Yes. Why are you home so late anyway?

I had a lot of work to do.

He said, Did you help the person you were trying to help?

I'm afraid not, amigo. I tried, though.

He said, Dada, I'm a little sad.

Me too, amigo.

Will you sleep with me for five minutes?

Sure I will. Scoot over.

■   ■   ■

TWENTY MINUTES LATER I walked downstairs. Katya said, I'm sorry about Winston.

Thank you.

I sat down next to her on the sofa. The TV was muted. She said, Your clients are not the only people who need you.

I said, I know.

■   ■   ■

LIFE IS EASIER with pillars. Mine are my family. One wife, one son, one dog. When I tell Katya that, she can't decide whether to believe me. Belief is a decision, I say; it doesn't just happen. Believe what I am telling you.

Before I met her, I planned to live out in the country. Get forty acres, run some cows, sit on the deck with the dog, watch the sun set and then come up, drive to my office at the university twice a week, come home, take a walk down to the creek. Read a lot of books, stick my head in a hole and say screw you to the world, have a conference call every morning with the lawyers I work with, file my appeals from a laptop eighty miles from death row.

To get to the piece of property I almost bought, you'd head west from Houston on I-10 toward San Antonio and get off the interstate at the small town of Sealy. Eric Dickerson went to Sealy High School. He's a Hall of Fame running back. There's a billboard at the exit reminding you of that. Dickerson played for the Los Angeles Rams in the 1980s. One day in practice the head coach, John Robinson, criticized Dickerson for not working hard. Dickerson said he was working hard. Robinson told him that if he was really working, he'd be sprinting on the running plays instead of just jogging. Dickerson said, I am running, Coach. Robinson went out onto the field and ran next to him. Well, he tried to.

From a distance, ease can easily be mistaken for indifference.

■ ■ ■

STORIES OF EXECUTIONS are not about the attorneys. They're about the victims of murder, and sometimes their killers. I know death-penalty lawyers who are at the movies when their clients get executed. I know one who found out on Thursday that his client had been executed on Monday. He'd been scuba diving in

Aruba. I understand that. It's possible to care without seeming to. It's also possible to care too much. You can think of yourself as the last person between your client and the lethal injection, or you can see your client as the person who put himself on the rail to that inevitability. One is healthier than the other.

My first client was executed in 1989. Derrick Raymond was an average bad guy who did one very bad thing. He dropped out of high school in tenth grade. Two years later he enlisted in the army to learn a skill. He wound up in Vietnam. He did not talk much to me about the war. I learned about his service record ten years after he was executed, when one of his army buddies tried to track him down but got in touch with me instead. Derrick returned to Houston with a purple heart and a heroin habit that cost him five hundred dollars a week, but still without any job skills. He pumped gas until he got fired for missing too many days. Drug addiction has many consequences. He started robbing convenience stores and fast-food restaurants. After one stickup, which netted him $73 and change, he was running down the street when the security guard gave chase, shooting. One shot hit Derrick in the leg. He fell to the pavement, turned around, and fired five shots at the security guard. The guard took cover, but one shot hit a seven-year-old boy who had just finished having lunch with his mother. There might be nothing sadder than dead children. On top of that, Derrick was black and the boy was white. That's a bad combination. The jury took less than two hours to sentence him to death.

Derrick's lawyer fell asleep during the trial—not just once, but repeatedly. The prosecutor was appalled, but the trial judge just sat there. When a new lawyer requested a new trial, the court of appeals said no, because the judges believed Derrick would have been convicted even if his lawyer had been awake. Another court-appointed lawyer represented him for his habeas corpus appeals in state court. That lawyer missed the filing deadline. If you miss a deadline, the court will not consider your arguments. That's when I got appointed to represent Derrick in federal court. But the federal courts have a rule: They refuse to consider any issues that the state courts have not addressed first. The state court had said that Derrick's lawyer was too late and had therefore dismissed his arguments. So the federal court would not hear our appeal either.

My job as a lawyer, therefore, consisted mostly of planning the disposition of Derrick's estate. Of course, he didn't have an estate, meaning that my job was to arrange for the disposal of his body. (He did not want to be buried in a pauper's grave right outside the prison gates in Huntsville, Texas.) Making funeral arrangements didn't take very long either, so my job was really just to be his counselor, to listen to him, to send him books or magazines, to be sure he would not have to face death alone. My goal is to save my clients, but that objective is beyond my control. All I can control is whether I abandon them.

I would visit Derrick once a week and talk to him by phone another day. He had a son, Dwayne, who was twelve when his dad arrived on death row and nineteen when Derrick was executed. I sat next to them as they struggled to connect. The Internet is ruining society because human relationships are inherently tactile. It's hard to become close to a man you can't touch, even (maybe especially) if he's your dad. I told them I was hopeful that the Board of Pardons and Paroles and the governor would commute Derrick's sentence, and I was. I am always hopeful. Nothing ever works out, but I always think that it's going to. How else could you keep doing this work? I watched his execution because he asked me to.

At 12:37 a.m. on Thursday, March 9, 1989, Derrick was put to death in front of me, Dwayne, and two local reporters. Afterward, I hugged Dwayne, got in my truck, and drove with my dog and a case of Jack Daniel's to my cabin on Galveston Island. I sat on the deck watching the Gulf of Mexico and drinking. The moon was bright. The mullet were jumping in schools and I could see trout in wave curls feeding. I smelled the rain. I left the front door open so the dog could go outside when she needed to and dumped a week's worth of food in her bowl. At dawn the sky blackened and the storm rolled in. I made sure my lounge chair was under the eave then closed my eyes and slept. When I'd wake up to use the toilet, I'd drink a shot of whiskey and chase it with a pint of water. I intended not to get dehydrated. Other than the birds and the surf, the only sound I heard was the thump of newspapers landing on driveways every morning. On Monday, I opened four papers, to figure out what day it was. I ran for an hour on the beach with the dog and swam for thirty minutes in the surf while the dog watched. Walking back to the cabin for a shower I said to her, Sorry for being a terrible master. She picked up a piece of driftwood and whipped her head back and forth.

We had lunch sitting on the deck at Cafe Max-a-Burger. I ordered four hamburgers, a basket of onion rings, and a lemonade. The dog ate her two burgers so fast that I gave her one of mine. When I paid the bill the cashier said, That's one lucky dog.

I said, Thanks for saying so, but you have it backwards. That dog is by far my best quality.

■　■　■

I HEADED BACK to Houston. My original interest in the death penalty was entirely academic, not political or ideological, and at the time Derrick got executed, I was working on a project examining the comparative competency of lawyers appointed to represent death-row inmates in Texas, Florida, Virginia, and Kentucky. I was scheduled to meet with an assistant who was helping me collect data. Traffic on the Gulf Freeway was going to make me late. Driving recklessly, I sideswiped an elderly woman near the NASA exit. I jumped out of my truck and was apologizing before my feet hit the pavement. She screwed up her face like she'd just swallowed sour milk. She said she was going to call the police. I told her I wasn't drunk, I just smelled like it. She smiled and said, I believe you, young man.

The law school has blind grading. Students identify themselves on their final exam with a four-digit number. Every year I hire as research assistants the three numbers who write the best answers. When I asked Katya to work for me, I didn't even know her name.

An unwritten rule forbids teachers from dating students. I think violations of that rule can be forgiven if you ultimately marry them. A week after Derrick's execution, I finally got up the nerve to ask Katya out.

We ate dinner at Ninfa's on the east side. It was back in the days when the east side was iffy at night. We sat in the back. She said, You have sad eyes.

I think you're most alive when you're sad.

That's bullshit.

My favorite moment in the old *Mary Tyler Moore Show* is when Mary interviews for the job in the WJM newsroom. Lou Grant says to her, You've got spunk. She beams with pride and says, Well, yes. He says, I hate spunk.

I told her about Derrick. She asked whether I would represent anyone else. I told her I thought I would.

I said, It seems like important work. I guess I don't think people should have to die alone, no matter what bad thing they did. She asked whether I thought it would make a difference. I said, Probably not.

She said, I think there's a word for trying to get in the way of something that's preordained.

Preordained is a little strong.

I thought, Besides, whether something is inevitable isn't the same as whether it's right, but I was feeling too old to say something so naive on a first date.

She smiled, which I interpreted as agreement. The server brought our food. I had ordered for both of us: tacos al carbon and ratones. She said, What are these?

I said, Rats.

Really.

Seriously. That's what they're called.

They were large jalapeño peppers, split open, stuffed with shrimp and Mexican cheese, dipped in batter, and deep-fried.

She took a bite, and her face broke out in a sweat. She said, These are delicious.

Here, I said, and I slid her my mug of beer.

She said, I think that if you're going to keep doing this, and it isn't going to matter, then you need a better coping strategy than a case of bourbon.

I said, That's probably true.

■ ■ ■

Most lawyers I work with would never marry a prosecutor. Some of them are making a big mistake. People use proxies to make judgments in life, but the problem with proxies is that most of them are often wrong. A few years ago Katya and I were eating breakfast at the Bellagio. James Carville was sitting by himself at the counter. Katya said, That is one marriage I don't understand.

I understand it. Party affiliation is not their proxy. They used something else.

I myself use books and dogs, and they have never led me astray. When Katya graduated from law school, I gave her a first edition of Walker Percy's *The Second Coming*. She read the first page and smiled. We were at my old house, sitting in the book-lined living room, listening to Frank Morgan. The dog normally didn't like women in the house. Katya patted the sofa and the dog, who weighed almost as much as she did, hopped up and lay down next to her. Katya scratched her under the jaw, and the dog purred like a kitten. Katya looked at me and said, She likes to be scratched, right here.

■　■　■

WHEN JEREMY WINSTON got executed, I had known him for only two months. I met him and Ezekiel Green, another death-row inmate, the same day, the date of Katya's and my tenth anniversary. Winston's lawyer had called me and said he wasn't going to do any more work on the case because he didn't have time. To his credit, at least he felt guilty about the fact that he was abandoning his client. You meet many crappy or lazy lawyers, but not very many who admit to others that they're crappy or lazy. He wondered whether my office would throw the Hail Mary pass. We're a nonprofit legal-aid corporation that does nothing but represent death-row inmates. I told him I'd talk to Winston the next time I was at the prison.

Winston was so fat he had to sit sideways in the cage where inmates visit with their lawyers. His arms were green, one solid tattoo from wrist to shoulder. In between each knuckle on each hand were tiny crosses. I introduced myself. He saw me staring at his hands. He said, Are you a religious man?

I'm afraid not.

He said, Not a problem. I didn't mean nothing by the question. Just asking.

I told Winston there was nothing left to do in his case. We could file a challenge to the method the state intended to use to execute him, but it was not likely to succeed.

He said, Yeah, I heard they're gonna kill me with some drug that they ain't allowed to use to kill animals, is that right?

One of the drugs that is part of the lethal injection combination has in fact been banned by veterinarians. Lawyers representing death-row inmates in some states had raised successful challenges to the lethal-injection cocktail protocol. So far, the legal maneuvering had not worked in Texas. But the lawyers in my office and I had a new idea, and we thought it might work in Winston's case. I was not going to tell him that.

I said, That is true, but it doesn't matter. Most of the judges don't really believe that you're going to suffer when you're executed, and even if they did, they probably wouldn't care, and even if they cared, they couldn't do anything about it. He nodded. I said, We can file a suit for you, but you will not win. If you want me to file it, though, I will. I just want you to know what's going to happen. I'll file it and we will lose.

I paused to let him ask a question. He didn't, so I continued, Not only will you not win, but besides that, you probably won't know for sure that you have lost until twenty minutes before the execution. That's when the Supreme Court clerk will call me. They like to wait as long as they can so that we don't have any time to file anything else. They'll call me and then I'll call you. Are you following me? He nodded. I said, What I'm telling you is that I think you are going to lose, and that after I call to tell you that we have lost, you're not going to have much time to prepare. Knowing all that, do you still want me to file it?

I knew as I was talking that I sounded almost cruel. That's not what I was aiming for. I was trying to sound completely without hope. I needed him to be hopeless. I didn't want him to be thinking he was going to win up until the time I called him. I didn't want there to be even the faintest glimmer of hope. I don't mind admitting that I know exactly whose interests I had at heart. I've called people who still had hope. It's easier to tell someone who is prepared to die that he is about to die. Winston said, That will be tough on Marie.

Who's Marie?

My wife. We got married last year. You didn't know that? I told him I didn't. She's sweet, from Louisiana. I nodded. Winston drummed his fingers against the glass that separated us. The Randy Newman song "Marie" started playing in my head: *You looked like a princess the night we met.* I listened, lost, while Winston thought. Finally he said, Yeah, go on ahead. You're the first dude that's been straight with me. Everybody's always sugarcoating everything. I'm tired, man, tired of being lied to. Do what you can do.

I told him I would and asked if he had any questions. He said, Yeah I do. Do you have any good news for me? He smiled.

I said, I'm seeing a guy named Ezekiel Green when I finish talking to you. Do you know him?

Winston said, Bald-headed skinny dude with a tattoo on his face?

I said, I don't know. I've never seen him.

He said, I think that's the guy. Something ain't right with him. They gassed him once and he didn't cough or choke or nothing. Just laughed. Talks to himself a lot. Dude showers with his boots on.

I said, Thanks. I'll send you what we file. I probably won't see you again. Take care, though, and I'll talk to you. He touched his hand to the glass between us. I touched it back.

15

■ ■ ■

MURDER IS PERHAPS the ugliest crime, which is why it is so shocking that most murderers are so ordinary in appearance. Average height, average weight, average everything. Even after all these years, some part of me expects people who commit monstrous deeds to look like monsters. I meet them, and they look like me.

I stare at their eyes or their hands and try to picture them doing the terrible deed. At the time, this was how I imagined it happened: She was sleeping on the sofa when she felt the gun barrel pressed against her temple. She would have thought it was one of the kids horsing around, except for the hiss of *shhhh*, followed by, Open your eyes, bitch. She did. Did she think she was dreaming? The gun looked like the one she took to the target range, and she wondered for a moment whether it was. That was the last thought she had. The killer fired one shot, killing her instantly.

He chose the small-caliber gun because it did not make a lot of noise. It would not disturb the neighbors, but it did get the attention of one of the children, who had been playing in another room. The killer looked up and saw him there. There weren't supposed to be any children. The boy looked to be around twelve, old enough to remember what he'd seen. The boy ran back into the bedroom. The killer walked toward the boy's retreat, blood dripping from the gun. The boy was on the floor, under the bed, cradling his little sister. The killer pressed the gun against the boy's chest, and fired one time. The little girl screamed. He pointed the gun at her heart and pulled the trigger again, and she was quiet.

16

On the day I met with Winston, I did not have time to meet with my client Henry Quaker, who had been sentenced to death for committing the triple murder. But his case was why I was at the prison. Ezekiel Green had written me a letter, saying he had important information that would prove Quaker was innocent. There are some letters I don't ignore.

■　■　■

GREEN WAS WAITING for me in the booth. He had an elaborate *E* tattooed on his right cheek and a *G* on his left. I introduced myself and addressed him as Green. He said, That's not my name no more. I changed it. I'm Shaka Ali. He paused and looked back over his shoulder, checking to make sure the guard was not standing behind him. He asked, Did you get my letter?

I told him that's why I was there.

He said, I know all about you. I read your book.

You don't hear much about people like Green from people like me. Most abolitionists like to focus on innocence. I see their point. They think as soon as we use DNA to prove with certainty that an innocent man has been executed—and that day will surely come—even the sheriffs and prosecutors down here in Texas will choose life.

But the book of mine Green said he read argued that even the guilty should be spared. I used to support the death penalty. I changed my mind when I learned how lawless the system is. If you have reservations about supporting a racist, classist, unprincipled regime, a regime where white skin is valued far more highly than dark, where prosecutors hide evidence and policemen routinely lie, where judges decide what justice requires by consulting the most recent Gallup poll, where rich people sometimes get away with murder and never end up on death row, then the death-penalty system we have here in America will embarrass you to no end.

Sometimes I think I became a lawyer because I believe rules matter, but I suppose I could have the cause and effect reversed. Either way, I said in that book that the abolitionists' single-minded focus on innocence makes them seem as indifferent to principle as the vigilantes are. I might have gone too far. One abolitionist group invited me to give a talk at their annual conference, then disinvited me after the head of their board realized who I was.

I don't know whether Green had really read my book, but if he had, I bet he would have liked it. It's about people like him: murderers who did exactly what the prosecutors said they did.

He said, You're an activist just like me. Did you know my old man helped organize factory workers?

I raised my eyebrows, trying to look impatient, which I was. I said, No, I didn't know that. I looked at my watch.

He said, I'm going to organize the guys in here. We can't stay locked up all day long, man. They treat us like animals. It's harassment. Captain wrote me up the other day for saying *fuck*. I got a right to free speech, man. I can say what I want. I been talkin' to the ACLU people about suing. They sued about the conditions in Mississippi and Oklahoma. Did you know that?

I did know that, but Green did not wait for me to answer. He kept on: They should let us work, listen to the radio, something, you know what I'm sayin'? His right eyelid pulsed like a cricket was trying to get out. He rubbed his hand across his shaved head. He smiled. His two front teeth were gold. He said, When I do this to my hair the guards know not to mess with me. No 'fro for them to grab ahold of. I'm ready to rumble, man. You know what I'm saying? I been keeping it like this for almost a year. They gas me when they take me to the shower, but it don't bother me none. I can hold my breath for twenty minutes. I wait till it's all gone.

I looked at my watch again. He said, You gotta be somewhere?

I told him that I had to get back to my office to get something filed. He asked, Who for? I shook my head and didn't answer. He said, Don't matter. It's good you came to see me. We need to be dialoguing. We can learn from each other. You got the book smarts. I know what's going down in here. I tell you, and we can take it on. You can come see me on a regular basis, all right?

He said, Can you get me something to eat?

Death row has several vending machines, filled with junk food and soda. People visiting inmates can buy them food by putting change into the machines, pushing the buttons, and letting the guard remove the items and pass them to the inmate. Visitors cannot bring paper money into the prison. The prison has a lot of rules. I told Green I didn't have any change.

Green had murdered two people. He said God had told him to do it. His lawyer asked the jury to rule that Green was insane. The jury said he wasn't, and the jury was right. Green knew the difference between right and wrong. He was not insane. He was just crazy.

I said, Can we talk about the letter? What do you know that can help me?

He said, Hold on, bro. You got to do something for me first. You got to earn my trust. Then he was off and talking again. He was talking about filing a civil-rights suit against the prison so he could get different medication and satellite radio. He said the only stations they could get were Christian talk shows. He said they were discriminating against the Muslims. He said they punished people arbitrarily. He said the guards let some inmates use cell phones in exchange for sex or bribes. A lot of what he was saying was probably true, but what he wanted was somewhat outside my expertise and way outside my interest. I looked at his face and pretended to listen. All I heard was blah blah blah blah blah. I heard him say, You hear what I'm sayin', bro?, and I felt myself nod. I was staring at the tattoos on his face, trying to figure out how to change the *E* into an *S*, seeing if I could find a way to make the *G* into an *A*. He must have asked me a question I didn't answer. He stood up and banged the phone against the window. He screamed, Are you listening to me? I stared at him. He banged the phone again and said, I don't even have to be talking to you, motherfucker, do I?

I said, No you don't, just like I don't have to be talking to you.

He said, Then get the hell out of here, motherfucker.

I have a confession to make. I had a pocket full of quarters. I do not like all my clients, and I did not like Green. He made the same mistake that death-penalty supporters routinely make. He assumed that because I represent guys like him, I must like guys like him. He assumed that because I am against the death penalty and don't think he should be executed, that I forgive him for what he did. Well, it isn't my place to forgive people like Green, and if it were, I probably wouldn't. I'm a judgmental and not-very-forgiving guy. You can ask my wife. I would have left midway through his tirade, except I wanted to know what he knew. It appeared he wasn't going to tell me, so I didn't have any more reason to stay. I stood up. I said, Have a nice life, asshole.

■　　■　　■

ON SEPTEMBER 1, the Sunday of Labor Day weekend, Katya and I got married at the Doubletree Hotel near the Houston Galleria. Three months earlier, we sat with the executive chef in his kitchen, sampling wines and tasting tuna, halibut, and loin of lamb. While we were deciding on our celebratory meal, the Quaker family was dying on the other side of town.

Dorris Quaker worked the third shift at Ben Taub General Hospital. That night, she made fried chicken and biscuits for her two children, twelve-year-old Daniel and Charisse, who was eight. Their next-door neighbor, Sandra Blue, sat at the table drinking sweet tea while the Quakers ate. Sandra said that she left at nine, when Dorris started getting the kids ready for bed. A few minutes later, Dorris called Sandra and told her she was going to take a short nap and leave for the hospital in an hour. She'd get home at seven thirty the next morning, just as the kids were waking up. Daniel knew to call Sandra if he needed anything, and Sandra knew to call Dorris. This had been their routine since Dorris and Henry had separated three months before.

At eight the next morning, Sandra went outside to pick up the newspaper. Dorris's car was in the driveway. The house was quiet. Sandra thought that the kids were watching TV and that Dorris was asleep. It was Labor Day. There wasn't any school. At eleven, she noticed the quiet again. No one answered when she knocked. The door was unlocked.

As soon as she saw Dorris lying on the sofa she dialed 911, then she walked into the back bedroom and found the children. When police arrived, Sandra was sitting on the floor in the children's bedroom, hugging her knees to her chest. A detective took her statement and sent her home.

■　■　■

On the drive back to Houston from the prison after seeing Green, my cell phone rang. It was Jeremy Winston's wife, Marie. Her voice was as thin as he was fat. She was calling to thank me for trying to help her husband. That was it, no other agenda. I've noticed that if you do the tiniest little thing for someone who has never received even the slightest kindness, you get rewarded with ridiculously effusive gratitude.

Katya handed me a glass of bourbon when I walked in the door. Happy anniversary, she said.

Shouldn't we be drinking champagne?

Yes, but taste that. It's a present.

I drank a swallow. Wow, I said. What did you pay for this?

Is it good?

Yes, I said. Amazing.

Then it was a steal. Come on, Lincoln's already in bed, waiting for his story. I told him we were going to dinner and that Nana was staying with him.

Lincoln was in bed reading Amelia Bedelia. His nanny, Maria, has been with us since Lincoln was six weeks old. He calls her Nana. He said, Hi, Dada. Do you know what a pun is?

I said, Yes, amigo. I love puns.

He said, Me too. Puns are fun, get it? He said, Tell me a real-life story, okay?

I said, Okay. When I was a little boy, just about your age, I read an Amelia Bedelia book. In the book I read, she cooked an egg on top of a car. I asked my dada whether you could really cook an egg on a car, and he said that you might be able to do it if it was hot enough outside. So the next Saturday, after my dada got home from playing tennis, I went outside, and while he was swimming I cracked an egg on the hood of his car.

What happened? Lincoln asked.

I said, It was a big mess. The egg got hard and stuck to the car. I had to clean it off, and my dada made me clean the whole car.

Even the inside?

Yep, even the inside. I didn't ever do that again.

Lincoln said, That's a funny story.

I said, Good night, amigo.

■   ■   ■

Wᴇ ᴀsᴋᴇᴅ ғᴏʀ ᴀ ᴛᴀʙʟᴇ in the back at Café Annie. I told Katya about my day. She said, You have to write him and apologize.

Apologize for what?

You told a man on death row to have a nice life.

The guy's an asshole. I'm not going to apologize.

The waiter brought our appetizers and a bottle of Veuve Clic-quot. We ordered a coffee-roasted sirloin and grilled redfish. I lifted my champagne glass to make a toast. Katya's eyes were wet.

What's the matter, K?

She said, The guy is totally messed up. He can't help the way he is. It's really bad karma for you to say that to him.

Bad karma? Are you serious? Can I tell you what the guy did?

I said, Green beat his pregnant wife to death with his fists. He had his five-year-old son with him watching while he did it. Then he drove with his son to his mother-in-law's house and strangled her, again with his little boy watching.

Katya started to say something. I said, Wait, I'm not finished. He drove to a motel, and when his boy fell asleep he left him there. Just left him. The next morning the kid woke up alone in the room and wandered outside looking for his dad. A maid found him. Green was arrested watching TV in his trailer at nine in the morning. He was on his sixth beer.

Katya ran her finger around the rim of her champagne glass. She said, I don't know how he got to be that way. But he was reaching out to you because he respects you. You can't leave it like that.

I said, I'm not going to apologize to him.

We sat silently. Our food arrived. I cut the steak and the fish in half, put some on each of our plates, and ate a piece of the meat. This is great, I said. Katya smiled. Sad and happy, all at once. I'm either in a good mood or, more often, a bad one. She is more complicated than I am. She can be in both. I said, I'll write him and thank him for seeing me. I won't apologize, but I'll write him. Okay?

Okay, she said. Thank you. And the sadness was gone, just like that.

I said, What was that bourbon, anyway?

Pappy Van Winkle. Twenty years old. I'm glad you liked it.

How many bottles did you buy?

Just one. It wasn't cheap.

I figured that. I guess I'll drink it slow.

We had coffee and cognac. I was remembering how Green looked at me as I was leaving. She said, Where did you go?

I told her I was thinking about what it would be like to live the rest of my life in a windowless space the size of my closet. I said, It might be a little easier if it was your closet.

Hah hah.

Katya practiced law for seven years. She was good at it, but she's too artistic, and too sincere, to be happy as a lawyer. So she went to art school and started teaching high-school photography. If it weren't for Lincoln, that's probably what she'd still be doing. But when our son arrived, she devoted herself with an intensity I had not seen before to being a mom and, far more daunting, to making me into a dad.

I was feeling sentimental, and when I'm feeling sentimental

I am triter than normal. I had never gotten around to my toast. I lifted my cognac glass. I said, You and our son are the best things in my life. Thank you.

Katya had heard this toast before. I had heard her response before. She said, It sure took you long enough to decide.

When you don't get married until late in life, the list of qualities you expect your wife to have can grow to be specific and long.

Katya is a competitive ballroom dancer. I bump into our piano walking from the kitchen to the library. She could have been a concert flutist, but her parents were practical Germans who saw no prospects in earning a living as a musician. My great-grandparents died in the Holocaust. The first time I met Katya's mom and dad I wondered where their parents had been.

I said, You were pretty much the exact opposite of the person my list described. It took me a little while to realize that maybe the list was wrong.

She said, *Maybe?*

I smiled. I said, A little while to realize that the list was definitely wrong.

She said, Maybe you should stop keeping lists.

■　■　■

THE NEXT MORNING I woke up before dawn and went for a run with the dog. I came home and brewed a pot of coffee for myself and a cup of tea for Katya. I made breakfast for Lincoln while Katya fixed his lunch and helped him get dressed. I showered and shaved and put on a suit. I usually wear blue jeans and a T-shirt to the office, so Lincoln asked me why I was dressed funny. I told him I had to go to a meeting. Katya said, Hey Linco, it's time to go to school. I kissed them both good-bye then drove to the courthouse.

I walked into the courtroom for the 175th Harris County District Court and chatted with Loretta, one of the clerks. I hadn't seen her since August, when my client Leroy Winter had been executed. Winter had been serving a prison sentence for sexual assault of a minor when he killed a guard. His defense was that the guard had been raping him. It might have been true, but it's still not a good idea to kill a guard. Loretta said she was sorry about Winter. She was lying. Her friends are cops. She was just being polite. I appreciated it. I said, Thanks, Loretta. She told me that my wife must have picked out my shirt and tie, because they matched. I smiled and told her that she knows me pretty well. I asked her to please call the prosecutor to let her know that I was there.

A few minutes later, the prosecutor came into the court. While we waited for the judge to arrive, we talked about our upcoming vacations. My wife and I are going white-water kayaking, I told her. Shirley told me that she and her husband were going to the Pacific Northwest. She asked how long I've been kayaking, and I asked her whether she'd been to Seattle before. Most of my colleagues don't like her, but Shirley and I get along just fine. Because I used to support the death penalty, it's not so hard for me to have sympathy for the misguided souls who still do.

I saw two former students of mine, now assistant district attorneys. They asked how things were going at the law school where I teach, and we chatted about their careers. The judge walked in, and a bailiff shouted for us all to rise. Defense lawyers and prosecutors milled around, trying to work out deals with each other, or just engaging in courthouse gossip. Criminal courtrooms, when there isn't a trial going on, are a lot like a Middle Eastern bazaar.

A man charged with drug possession stood before the judge, in between the prosecutor and his own lawyer, whom he had met less than five minutes earlier, and pleaded guilty. He had been through this ritual before. He was as calm as you would be if you were standing in line to pay a parking ticket. The judge sentenced him to time already served. The prosecutor and I asked the judge if we could approach the bench, and she told us we could. The prosecutor said that she and I had compared calendars, and we wanted to see if she planned to be in town on February 4. The judge glanced down at her calendar and said that she did. Shirley handed the judge an order. Without looking down, the judge signed it.

The order the judge signed is called a death warrant. Shirley and I had picked the day that my client would die. We planned the execution around our vacations. The warrant commanded the director of the Texas Department of Criminal Justice to place Henry Quaker, on February 4, "in a room arranged for the purpose of execution" and then to inject him with "a substance or substances in lethal quantity sufficient to cause [his] death" and to continue with the injection "until the said HENRY QUAKER is dead."

I paced in the hall while Shirley made me a copy of the order. I have been reading these boilerplate warrants for close to twenty years, but they still take my breath away. I called Jerome, who had left the office and was on the way to the prison to see Henry. Jerome would deliver the news in person. I don't like for my clients to learn from a letter or even by phone that a date has been chosen for their deaths. I realize that it's absurd. What difference does it make how you're told when you're going to die? None, probably. But we all have our little idiosyncrasies.

I got in my truck to drive to my office at the law school. You don't see many homeless people in Houston. They're there, of course, but unlike New York or San Francisco, where you have to hurdle them on the sidewalks, you can pretend like they aren't here, because they aren't in my neighborhood. But I see them when I'm at the courthouse. So I keep a stack of twenty or thirty one-dollar bills in my truck. The experts say that they're just going to buy booze. For all I know the experts are right, but I've never figured out why that means I shouldn't hand out the money. If I'd been alive five hundred years ago, and been a Catholic, of course, I'd have been one of the sinners buying indulgences.

There's one homeless guy, Stan, who lives with his three dogs and a grocery cart under the freeway where I turn left. How can you turn a blind eye to a man who shares the food he scavenges from Dumpsters with his dogs? He has a squeegee in his cart. I usually give him a dollar not to clean my windshield and Milk-Bones for the dogs. The first time I gave him money he asked me my name. I told him my friends call me Doc. He said, Cool, then I'll call you Doc. Some days I give him cans of tuna, or crackers and cheese. He says, This is nice, but I'd prefer some beer. Last Christmas I gave him a six-pack of Shiner. He said, Whoa. The good stuff. Thanks, Doc.

I saw Stan on the day the judge signed Quaker's death warrant. He said, Hey Doc, you've looked better. I nodded and gave him the whole stack of ones.

■   ■   ■

HENRY QUAKER'S STORY was treacly sweet. He and Dorris had been sweethearts at Yates High School. He carried her books to school, literally, and held her hand in the halls. They got married a week after they graduated, in 1983. Their son Daniel was born seven months later. Henry felt like he had to do something dramatic. He had a son on the way. He intended to support his wife and child, but he had been only a mediocre student. Although he loved to read, he had no skills and no prospects. So he enlisted in the army. It would be a living, and he figured he would get the job skills he needed to take care of his family. Dorris went to pharmacy school while they lived on the base, learning how to mix IVs. Henry learned heavy-machine maintenance and read a lot of books. They were a charming cliché. Charisse was born four years later. Henry served his time, became a reservist, and started welding in Houston. The pay was twice what he made as a soldier. He said he was deliriously happy. He would drink a beer after work with his buddies, but he was home in time to bathe the kids and put them to bed. On Saturday nights, he and Dorris paid a neighborhood kid to babysit, and they would go out to dinner and to the movies.

Then, in 1989, Henry was working at a chemical plant in Pasadena. Leaking gas ignited an explosion that measured over 3.0 on the Richter scale. You could feel the ground shake for miles. Henry escaped with barely a scratch, but his two best friends burned to death in a massive fire that took half a day to contain. Henry heard them screaming, first for help, then in agony. Their bodies were literally consumed by the flames.

A week later he was back on the job. Between the day he returned and the day his family was killed, Henry did not miss even a single day of work. But he stopped reading books and stopped going out for a beer after his shift. His coworkers described him as sullen and withdrawn. They said he did his work like he was hypnotized. No one could remember the last time Henry laughed or even smiled.

When police arrived at the Quaker house following the 911 call, Sandra Blue told them that Dorris and Henry had been separated for a few months. She said she didn't know him very well. He was quiet. When Sandra would see him in the mornings before he moved out, he was always polite, waved, said good morning, asked her how she was doing. He still spent a lot of time with the kids, shooting baskets, playing catch, going for ice cream. Even after they split, Henry came over to the house twice a week to pick up the kids. He adored them. Sandra had never seen or heard him yell at either of them, and she'd never seen or heard Henry and Dorris fighting.

She said there was no chance that Dorris was seeing some-one else. Henry was the love of her life.

Police found Henry at a construction site in the medical center. He was sitting astraddle a beam eleven stories up, welding. He was a suspect because the spouse is always a suspect. When police told him why they were there, he started to shriek.

He made more than $30,000 a year. He had good health insurance. When it looked like they were headed for divorce, he told Dorris that they should stay married until she found some-one else just so she and the kids could still be covered under his insurance, which was much better than the coverage Dorris had. The police asked Henry whether they could look inside his truck. He said that sure they could. A detective saw what he thought was blood. He read Henry his rights. A day later, the DNA lab reported that the blood was Daniel's.

■ ■ ■

AFTER WE CHOSE the date for Quaker's death I left the court-house and drove to my office at the law school. I asked my assis-tant to send an e-mail to my students saying I was canceling class. I closed my door and sat down to play poker. I entered a $2 tournament online. It took four and a half hours. I won $37. I poured myself a small Knob Creek and drove home.

Katya was in the kitchen making pasta for Lincoln, who was sitting at the table reading. He said, Hi, Dada. Katya looked at me and said, What's wrong?

I tried to make myself smile, but I couldn't. Lincoln said, Dada, did you give away all your money again?

When Lincoln was two I realized he was smarter than me. I said, Quaker's date is February fourth. Katya wrapped her arms around my shoulders.

Lincoln came over and circled his arms around my waist. Looks like it's time for a group hug, he said. I touched his hair, then his earlobe. He said, Mama, is the pasta ready yet? I'm hungry.

■　■　■

HENRY TOLD HIS TRIAL LAWYER, Jack Gatling, that he thought Dorris might have started seeing someone about six months before she was killed. He wasn't sure. He didn't know any more because he didn't ask. He didn't ask because he didn't want to know. He didn't want to know because whatever she was doing was his fault.

His lawyer asked him whether he was having an affair. Henry looked at him like he had a mouse hanging out of his mouth. He shook his head. Henry told Gatling that the only woman he had ever loved or slept with was Dorris. Gatling wrote the word *lovesick* on his legal pad. He doodled a broken heart. I had these pieces of paper in my file. When I showed them to Henry, he smiled. Henry told Gatling that Dorris first brought up the possibility of divorce two years before they separated. He answered, Whatever you want, baby. Dorris said, I want you to be the way you were. He said, I want that, too. I just don't know how. But he said that he would try. He told his lawyer, I might not have acted like it, but I loved my family. I could never have hurt them. Gatling put a question mark after *lovesick*.

The foreman at the job site where Henry had been working testified at the trial that Henry had been sullen. The man who lived next door to Sandra Blue, two doors down from the Quakers, told the jury that he saw a truck like Henry's in the driveway at around 8:00 p.m. He had given police the part of the license-plate number that he remembered. A DNA expert explained that the blood in Henry's truck belonged to his son. A police officer said that the three victims had been shot with a .22-caliber pistol, and that Henry owned such a gun. Officers looked in the house and in Henry's truck for the gun. It was never found. Someone from the benefits office of Henry's company showed the jury copies of the forms where Henry had listed himself as the beneficiary on life insurance policies taken out for his wife and kids; he stood to receive half a million dollars for their deaths. Gatling, Henry's lawyer, did not call any witnesses of his own. He told the jury that the case against Henry was entirely circumstantial. It was, of course, but Gatling had not challenged or questioned any of the circumstances. Saying he phoned it in would flatter him. Despite all that, it took the jury more than six hours to convict.

At the punishment phase of the trial, where the prosecutor asks the jury to sentence the defendant to death while the defense pleads for life, Gatling called no witnesses. He had not interviewed anyone from Henry's past who could have told the jury about him. He later said that he had been expecting an acquittal, so he wasn't prepared for sentencing. Henry told Gatling that he wanted to testify himself, but Gatling told him it would be a bad idea, and Henry went along. Gatling did not make a closing argument. He later said that he decided not to beg for Henry's life because by saying nothing, he would not give the prosecutor an opportunity to make a rebuttal. The judge said it was the only capital-murder trial she had ever heard of where the defense lawyer did not implore the jury to spare his client from execution. It took the jury three hours to sentence Henry to death.

■ ■ ■

I READ THE TRANSCRIPT of the trial after a federal judge appointed me to represent Henry in his federal appeals. As Yogi Berra said, it was déjà vu all over again. Gatling was dead, having died from cirrhosis of the liver, but his tactics in the trial had been exactly the same as his approach in the trial of Derrick Raymond, my first client. He did not interview any witnesses. He did not put on any evidence of his own. He had no idea whom the state was going to call as witnesses. Henry told me that Gatling smelled like a bottle at eight in the morning. He told me that Gatling fell asleep during the trial, and the judge's law clerk confirmed it was true.

Quaker's case was like my first client's in another way as well. The lawyer who had represented Quaker in his first appeal in state court had neglected to complain about the inadequacies of the trial lawyer. Quaker's lawyer did not miss a filing dead-line, but he might as well have. He did not raise a single decent claim, even though there were plenty to choose from. That was a problem; as I noted before, the federal courts will not consider any issue that the state court did not examine. The state court had not examined whether Quaker's trial lawyer was incompetent because the lawyer who represented him dur-ing that appeal failed to raise it. In other words, Gatling was not the last bad lawyer in the case. Quaker's appellate lawyer was incompetent, too. I would try again to go back to state court to complain about Gatling's incompetence, but the state courts have a rule of their own: Unless you raise the issue the first time, you cannot raise it later. So I was going to be ham-strung. The federal court would refuse to look into the issue because the state court had not examined it, and when I asked the state court to examine the issue so that I could go to fed-eral court, the state court would refuse because Quaker's origi-nal lawyers forgot to ask them to. I told Quaker that I wasn't optimistic.

He said, It's like a Catch-22, right? I nodded. He said, I love that book.

Normally, the first thing a death-penalty appellate lawyer does is conduct a complete investigation of the case: locate wit-nesses the previous lawyers had not talked to, interview jurors, reconstruct the entire case. But there was no point to doing that investigation without first figuring out a way to make it matter. Why spend a thousand hours pursuing futility? Death-penalty lawyers have many clients, and we have the same twenty-four hours in our day as everyone else. An hour spent on one case is an hour not spent on another. Jerome thought there was enough doubt about Henry's guilt that we should at least do enough to raise questions about his innocence. If we did that, perhaps a court would cut us some slack. I overruled him. It did not make sense to look for a needle in a haystack without even knowing whether a needle was in there. Instead, we would try to get a court to agree to let us start over. Then, we still might not find anything, but at least we would know that if we did find something, a court would listen.

So we filed papers in federal court saying that Henry had been represented at his trial by an incompetent trial lawyer, and that the only reason that issue had not been presented to the state appellate court was that his appellate lawyer was terrible, too. We said that basic fairness dictated that he should be entitled either to have the federal court address his issues, or to a second trip through the state courts so that the state court could address his issues. The federal judges said, in effect, Sorry, our hands are tied. We tried the same argument again, this time in state court. The state judges said, Sorry, the legislature has decided that you get one and only one crack, and you have had yours.

Nothing worked. Henry would not get a bona fide appeal, where some judge reviewed the legality of his trial. Jerome said, I still think we should investigate the innocence angle. If he didn't do it, someone will care about that.

I said, His kid's blood was in the car. He had a life insurance policy on his family. His gun, which is the same caliber as the murder weapon, is missing. There are no other suspects. How do you plan to prove that he's innocent?

Gary and Kassie looked at Jerome. He said, All I'm saying is that it's all we've got.

He did have a point.

A week after the federal appeals court had ruled against us, I saw one of the judges outside a restaurant, waiting for the valet to bring his car around. He had written the opinion in the case ruling against Quaker. He's a handwringer, a supposedly devout Catholic who goes to extraordinary lengths to uphold death sentences. I used to divide my life into boxes, too. I had different sets of friends who did not know each other, and all of them knew a different side of me. I'm sympathetic to people whose lives are segmented by Chinese walls. I understand this judge. He reminded me of who I used to be unhappy being. I stood behind him, hoping he might not notice me, but as his car arrived, he did. A tiny man, he hugged me, and his arms didn't get past my shoulders. He said, I saw Sister Helen Prejean give a speech last week. I have never been so moved in my life. What an amazing woman. He got in his car, waved, and drove away.

Sister Helen gave a speech at the law school where I teach a few years before. People were sitting in the aisles. She talked for more than an hour without a single note. She combines humility and moral authority in a way I'd never seen. Like the Houston Oilers head coach Bum Phillips used to say about Earl Campbell, she might not be in a class of her own, but it doesn't take long to call the roll. Afterward, several of us went out for a few drinks. It was the first time I went drinking with a nun. She said, You know, support for the death penalty is a mile wide, but just an inch deep. I believe that.

I said, Well, Sister, I believe you can drown in an inch of water. She cackled like a barnyard hen.

Three months later, I got a postcard in the mail. The Supreme Court had refused to hear our appeal.

◼   ◼   ◼

QUAKER WAS DOUR the day I went to tell him. Like nearly everyone, he had gotten his hopes up. I tried, but my efforts to squash his spirits had not entirely succeeded. The problem is, if you have an ember of hope, a desperate observer will perceive it and stoke it and fan it and cling to it no matter what you say. This is not simply human nature. It is the will to live. I talked legalese so I would not have to have an actual conversation. I said that our claims had been defaulted in state court and that we had not been able to exhaust them; I said that the state court ruled against us on independent and adequate state-law grounds, so the federal court lacked jurisdiction to address the merits; I said that the Supreme Court was not interested in the manner in which the procedural barriers interfered with his substantive rights. I paused. Quaker shook his head, like he was getting out of a pool. He said, I would never ever have killed my family.

The only thing worse than being gutless is feeling guilty about it. I could barely look at the guy.

Quaker had claimed to be innocent from the time I first met him. I had not paid much attention. It's hard to prove that someone is innocent. Where were you at eight o'clock on a Thursday night ten years ago? I had pinned my hopes on getting a judge interested in how unfairly Quaker had been treated. I had a good reason for telling Jerome that we were not going to waste time and money on innocence. I thought that even though I could not prove that he didn't do it, I could prove he would never have been convicted if he'd had a competent lawyer. But I hadn't been able to solve the procedural maze that prevented us from raising that argument. So now I had nothing left.

Well, almost nothing. When there's one arrow still left in the quiver, I believe I should fire it, even though it's too dull to do any damage. They can execute my clients, but I can make their job harder. Some lawyers call this throwing sand in the gears. I call it doing my job. My goal is to save my clients' lives. If I fail, I don't want it to be because there was gas left in the tank. It helps that I also didn't think Quaker should be executed, even if he did kill his wife and kids. I'm not sure why I thought that. You can't get any lower than people who hurt children. But we don't always choose what we think.

I said, I can file another appeal in state court claiming that you are innocent, but it will be impossible to prove. We'll lose, but we can give it a shot.

He said, Don't even bother, man. I asked him what he meant. He said, I ain't ever gonna get out of here until I'm dead, right? So I'm just ready to be done with it. I told him that if he was asking me to waive his appeal, I couldn't do that without having a psychologist examine him. I was bluffing. He didn't have any appeals left. He said, You have a family, right? I waited. He said,

Would you want to be alive if they were all dead and everybody thought you killed them?

■   ▦   ▓

FROM THE TIME I was in eighth grade until I was a senior in college, I was never full. I would eat hamburgers and ice cream for breakfast. In high school, we would go off campus for lunch to all-you-can-eat pizza buffets, and I would eat fifteen or twenty slices of pizza, along with half a dozen pieces of fried chicken. Other days I would eat four double-meat hamburgers from Burger King, with two orders of fries and an order of onion rings, or eight chili dogs from James Coney Island. After school and before dinner, I would eat half a dozen tacos. In college we would eat on weekends at an all-you-can-eat steak place next door to Houston's most famous strip club, and I would eat six or seven steaks, a baked potato, a salad, and a loaf of bread. Sundays my housemate and I would go to a pizza restaurant and order four large pizzas, two for him and two for me. During summer vacation, my brothers and I would stay up until dawn talking; I would sit down with a half-gallon tub of Blue Bell ice cream in my lap and a spoon. I was five foot ten and weighed 165 pounds.

When I was growing up, my parents kept a kosher home. For the eight days of Passover, there was no bread in the house. During my junior year of high school I got hungry in the middle of the afternoon on the third day of Passover. I drove to Jack-in-the-Box and ordered a triple-meat hamburger and four tacos.

My plan was to eat the food on the way home. There would be no evidence of my infraction. I finished the tacos and started on the burger. Three blocks from my house, a car ran a red light. I slammed on the brakes. Lettuce, pickles, onions, tomatoes, ketchup, and taco sauce went everywhere. I pulled over and picked pieces of shredded lettuce from the car's carpet. When my mother asked me where I had been, I said the library.

That night at dinner I said I was not very hungry. I had not not been hungry in many years. Guilty people, I have noticed, say and do inexplicable things.

On the drive home from the prison, I called the office and told Jerome he had been right. I asked him to write up the best argument we had for proving that Quaker was innocent.

■ ■ ■

Two days after my visit with Quaker, I received two letters from the prison. One was from Ezekiel Green. As I had promised Katya, I had written to thank him for seeing me. And as usual, Katya had been right. Green apologized for losing his temper. He said his medication wasn't right and he was always on edge. He asked me to come see him again.

The other letter was from Quaker. He wrote, I know this is hard for guys who do what you do, but it's what I want. I hear from the guys here that you represented Van Orman. Van Orman is a cool dude, real mellow. Congratulations on that, but I don't want to be like him, you understand? I hope you won't be mad.

I did understand. Van Orman was sent to death row for stabbing a pizza delivery man to death. Police caught him because he bought beer at a neighborhood bar with a $10 bill wet with fresh blood. An execution date was set. A judge appointed us to represent Van Orman at a trial where the sole issue would be whether he is mentally retarded. He is. He can't count change, tie his shoelaces, or boil a pot of water. He could not read a street map if his life depended on it. Van Orman is big and gentle and so obviously retarded that even the district attorney simply went through the motions in saying that he wasn't, and when the judge agreed with us, the district attorney didn't appeal.

But that's not what Quaker was referring to.

In the course of our investigation, we also learned that Van Orman didn't commit the murder. He was at the scene, but he didn't stab the driver, and he didn't have any clue that it was going to happen until it was all over. He thought he and two buddies were going to eat pizza and watch a baseball game. Then the doorbell rang, and one of the other guys stabbed the driver and brought the pizza and the driver's wallet inside. Massive Van Orman helped his friend put the dead driver back in his car. At the trial, we introduced evidence that Van Orman is innocent. One of the bailiffs came up to me after the proceedings were over and shook my hand and said he believed that the judge should order Van Orman released from prison. But that's not what the trial was about; it was about whether he's mentally retarded, and we proved that Van Orman is. So he got moved off of death row.

That's why Quaker congratulated me, and this is why he said he doesn't want to be like him: In place of the death sentence,

Van Orman will spend the rest of his life in prison for a crime he didn't commit.

But I'm a death-penalty lawyer and Van Orman won't get executed, so I count it as a victory. One of my clients committed suicide a week before his execution. That's a victory. Another died of AIDS. A victory.

My client Randy Baze is not on death row anymore, either. He was seventeen when he and two buddies hijacked a car, killing its owner. I was in the middle of losing one appeal after another in his case when the Supreme Court agreed to decide whether the states can execute people who were younger than eighteen when they committed murder. After the Court ruled in our favor, Baze tried to stay on death row anyway. He didn't want to move. He knew that if he moved to the general prison population, he would fall to the bottom of my to-do list, just like Van Orman, and he was right. He has compelling legal issues in his case, but they are not matters of life and death, not anymore. I can't even remember what they are.

One day, if I have some extra time, I'll go back to court to win Van Orman's and Baze's total vindication.

If I have some extra time.

■   ■   ■

I WALKED IN THE DOOR and poured myself a glass of the expensive bourbon Katya had bought me for our anniversary. She was drinking wine.

She said, Do you deserve the good stuff today?

I think I do, I said. Nobody got killed.

She said, For a change. We clinked our glasses together. She said, I picked up a chicken for you to roast. And Lincoln wants you to be sure to save the wishbone.

From the library Lincoln said, Hi, Dada. Mama said you would save the wisher bone for us to break in the morning when I have my breakfast. I said that sounded fine. He said, Will you read me a book now?

The three of us climbed the stairs to his room. After a book and a bedtime story, before Katya and I told him good night, I said, Hey amigo, what are you going to wish for if you get the bigger piece of the wishbone tomorrow?

He said, I'm not supposed to tell you, but I will anyway. I'm going to wish that I have a great life. And guess what, Dada? My wish already came true.

■   ■   ■

I TOLD KATYA about Quaker's letter. She said, You can't force him to appeal if he doesn't want to.

I said, Actually, I think I can. He doesn't have the right to let the state execute him for a crime he didn't commit.

She said, How are you going to prove that he's innocent?

Good question, I said. I told her about Quaker's reference to Van Orman.

She said, Van Orman is incapable of living outside an institution. If he weren't in prison, he'd be in some other facility, or homeless. You didn't betray him. You gave him the best life you could.

I said, There's been a load of compromisin' on the road to my horizon.

She said, Thanks for not singing it. Can we eat now?

■　■　■

IN APRIL 1972, I was twelve. My Little League team, the Mets, played the Pirates in the championship game. Our pitcher was the only twelve-year-old in the league who could throw a slider. Lots of kids could throw a curveball, but Andrew Peters could throw a bona fide slider. He went to junior college to play baseball. He got drafted his sophomore year, dropped out, and pitched two years in the minor leagues before he ruined his arm and gave up on his dream and joined the Marines. He was killed in the first Gulf War. I know this because his son Timothy goes to law school where I teach, and he told me last week when he came by my office to introduce himself.

I was the catcher on the Mets. Andrew was the coach's son. The Peters family lived one street behind mine. When Andrew would make an error during a game, Coach Peters didn't say anything. But at night, I would hear him screaming through the window.

Coach Peters would call the pitches. He sent me a signal, and I would relay it to Andrew. It was the bottom of the last inning.

They were batting. We were ahead 2–1. Their first hitter leaned out over the plate and got hit on the arm. Coach Peters was shouting at the umpire from the dugout that the player had walked into the pitch, but the umpire sent him to first base anyway. Their best hitter was next. Andrew threw two quick strikes. Coach Peters signaled a slider, and Andrew threw a beauty, right on the outside corner. The umpire called it a ball. Coach Peters raced out of the dugout screaming. The vein on the side of his neck looked like a dancing Gummi Bear. A short man, he had been an NCAA wrestling champion. There were pictures of him holding trophies hanging on the walls of their house.

The umpire just stood there. Coach Peters walked back to the dugout, kicking at the dirt. When he got there he must have said something I didn't hear, because the umpire pulled off his face mask, looked at Coach, and said, Cool it, Drew. Coach Peters picked up a bat and stared at the umpire. It seemed like a long time went by. Then he started walking toward the plate. The other team's third-base coach tried to cut him off. Coach Peters swung the bat, and I heard the other coach's ribs crack. Then there was mayhem. All the coaches, on their team and ours, and all the umpires jumped on Coach Peters. Years later I would recall the scene when watching videos showing five-man teams of helmeted prison guards rushing into a cell on death row to subdue one of my clients. They held Coach Peters there until two policemen arrived. The police put handcuffs on him and took him away. Andrew was crying hysterically, screaming, Daddy, Daddy, Daddy. Coach Peters didn't turn around. He sat in the backseat of the squad car for an hour, until the police let him go.

Timothy said, My dad was friends with Henry Quaker. Before Dad went back to Iraq, Mr. Quaker helped him find a job. Timothy pronounced it "eye-wrack." He said, Mr. Quaker had dinner at our house a few times. He would always bring me a book. I don't believe Mr. Quaker did what they said he did. Timothy told me who his dad was. He said, You knew my dad, didn't you? I told him we had grown up together, that we played ball on the same team. He said, I hear through the grapevine that you use students on your cases. If you need some students to help on Mr. Quaker's case, I volunteer. I told him I'd think about it.

■ ■ ▓

DEPENDING ON WHOM you ask—Katya or me—we dated for somewhere between seven and two years before getting engaged. She teases me about why it took me so long. It's because she's exactly the type of person I never thought I'd marry. She's beautiful, athletic, artistic, and understanding. I'm bookish, plodding, and unforgiving. Falling in love with her created in me a cognitive dissonance that took awhile to subside. I'm not a good enough writer to know how to say this without sounding corny, but the day I decided to propose was the day I realized I would never run out of things I wanted to talk to her about and I would never get tired of looking at her. Two and a half years into our marriage, she got pregnant.

We were not trying not to have a kid, but we were not trying to have one, either. We liked our life. We saw a movie or two every week, we went to bars and restaurants, we talked about books. Once a month or so, Katya would go out dancing. (That she would do without me; as Dirty Harry said, a man has got to know his limitations.) We'd read stories from the newspaper to each other over breakfast.

The night we learned about Lincoln, we saw *American Beauty* before meeting three other couples for dinner. We drank many martinis. At two in the morning, Katya was sick. She threw up food, then gastric juices, then dry heaves, then red foamy blood. I was terrified. She was too exhausted to be scared. I drove us to the hospital. Katya vomited twice more, walking from the car to the admitting area. Before we had finished filling out the paperwork, the nurse said, Kidney stone, sweetheart. Have you had them before?

They ran a sedative and an antinausea medicine through her IV. Her eyes slid shut. I asked whether I could have something. The nurse smiled. She thought I was joking. I said, Really.

At four the doctor walked in, glanced at her chart, and said he was virtually certain it was a kidney stone. But they would do an X-ray anyway, just to be sure. I felt myself sag with relief. They were wheeling her out of the cubicle when a nurse walked in with a piece of paper and stopped the doctor. He looked down and smiled like he was in a movie. Apparently, a routine pregnancy screen is part of the protocol. He said, Congratulations.

Two months after Lincoln was born, I had an argument in the court of appeals. The Sunday before I left for New Orleans, we were sitting on a bench in Hermann Park watching the paddleboats. You could feel the first hint of autumn. The air was thick with smoke from charcoal fires, and the smell of hamburgers grilling made me hungry. I was trying to get a new trial for an illegal immigrant because the prosecutors had kept all the blacks and Hispanics off the jury. My client had murdered a pregnant woman and her fourteen-year-old daughter. Those facts had absolutely nothing to do with the legal issues in the appeal, but there was no way the judges would overlook them. I was thinking, I've got no chance of winning this case.

Winona was lying at our feet. Lincoln was in a jogging stroller. Katya was pushing him forward, pulling him back. She was looking out at the water. She said, If you are not going to be with us when you're with us, you might as well stay home.

■ ■ ■

WHEN LINCOLN WAS NEARLY TWO, I was making coffee in the kitchen one morning while Katya was getting him dressed. She called down to me to turn on the *Today* show. There on TV, talking to Katie Couric, was Lana Norris, the mother of Clay Peterson. Clay Peterson was dead. He had been murdered during a robbery of a convenience store by my client Johnny Martinez. Martinez had stabbed him eight times. The murder was caught on the store's security camera, so Clay Peterson's mother had watched a video of her son bleeding to death. She told me she had watched it at least a hundred times. It made her feel like she was close to her son, with him, as he lay dying. Norris was on TV because it was sweeps week on television, and she was a curiosity. A deeply religious person whose son had been saving money to study for the ministry when his life was cut short, Norris had met with Martinez for nearly four hours a week before his scheduled execution. After the meeting, Ms. Norris wrote a letter to the governor of Texas urging that Martinez's life be spared.

Martinez's own mother was a heroin addict who sold her kids' possessions to support her drug habit. His neighbor made him masturbate while he filmed it. I think the video is still on the Internet. No court of law ever took Johnny away from his mother, but she couldn't have been more absent. Martinez was raised by his grandmother. Lana Norris told me at the prison after her meeting with Johnny ended that she did not want Martinez's grandmother to lose a child and be forced to go through what she had gone through herself. She told Katie Couric the same thing.

The governor in Texas cannot grant a reprieve unless the parole board authorizes him to. By a vote of 8–7, the board voted against commuting Martinez's sentence from death to life in prison. One of the board members who voted in the minority called me to tell me the result of the vote before it was announced. He told me not to tell anyone that he had called. It was a breach of protocol. I could hear him softly crying.

Two hours before the execution I sat with Martinez in the holding cell. When the parole board member had called me the day before, he said, I just want to tell you that I do not think Mr. Martinez should die. I've been reading these petitions for ten years, hundreds of cases, and this is the first time I've voted to spare a life. I am impressed with who Mr. Martinez has become. I wish I could have convinced one more person. I really do. I'm sorry, sir. I repeated this conversation to Martinez. He nodded twice and stifled a sob. He said, It doesn't make any sense, but I feel better that not everybody wants to kill me.

I was going to be witnessing the execution with his brother and sister. He did not want his mother there, but he asked me to be sure to tell her that he loved her. He knew his brother would not convey the message. The guard said it was time to go. Johnny's hands were cuffed together and then shackled to a leather belt around his waist. He tried to lift his hand to shake mine. I hugged him and told him that I wished I had done more. He said, You did everything. You were the only one. Now go right home when you leave this hell and hug your son, okay? Hug Lincoln until he falls asleep tonight, will you? I had never told Martinez my son's name. I'm not sure how he learned.

I said I would, but when I got home from watching Martinez die, Lincoln was already sleeping. I carried him from his bed into Katya's and my bedroom and hugged him until I fell asleep myself. I thought that was close enough.

■ ■ ■

I WRITE DOWN MY DREAMS because they scare me. They scare me because I understand them.

The night Martinez got executed, I dreamed Lincoln and I were in a hotel room, waiting for room service. He opened the window. It was cold outside. I said, Close it, Lincoln. He ignored

52

me and climbed out onto the ledge. He threatened to jump. Go ahead, I said. He looked at me, wounded. On the television the hotel safety video was playing on a loop, warning people not to use the elevators in case of a fire. I put my hand on the small of Lincoln's back, meaning to hook my fingers through his belt, but before I could, he jumped. I heard only silence as he fell. Then a splash. He had fallen into the hotel pool. By the time I got downstairs, Lincoln was clinging to the side, and Katya was already there. I woke up, covered with sweat.

It was nearly 3:00 a.m. I started to shiver violently and could not go back to sleep. I put on a sweatshirt and checked to make sure Lincoln was fine. I kissed Katya on the cheek, went into the kitchen, and poured myself a drink. The dog thought it was time to go out. She followed me downstairs. But when she looked outside and saw it was still dark, she climbed back up the stairs and hopped into bed. I carried my drink into our library and, one by one, deleted all the Martinez files from my computer.

It is easier to forget failure if you don't have the icons to remind you.

■   ■   ■

IN *THE INTERPRETATION OF DREAMS*, Freud sides with those who maintain *conscience is silent in our dreams....Ethical indifference reigns supreme.* He was wrong, at least about me. In my dreams my conscience shouts until it wakes me and makes me too afraid to go back to bed. If you don't want to be confronted with an aerial map of all the corners you've cut that day, you shouldn't go to sleep.

Katya and I had invited three couples over for dinner later that week. Two of my clients had been executed in the past ten days. She asked if I wanted to cancel. I said no. Cooking relaxes me. I pan-roasted a loin of venison with lots of thyme and garlic, and I deep-fried cauliflower dipped in beer batter. Over cocktails we were talking about the JonBenet Ramsay murder. Like everyone else, I suspected the mother. Our friend Sharon disagreed. She believed the intruder theory. She and her husband Tom are oncologists. We compared the futility of our work. Sharon said, My goal is to save my patients' lives. Barring that, my goal is to extend their lives as long as I can. If I can't do that either, at least I can struggle with them for as long as they have.

I said, Exactly. Me too.

Except my clients killed somebody. She asked me why I keep doing it. I paused to consider the answer. Katya said, Because he's wracked with guilt when he even contemplates stopping, and he thinks doing anything else would be unfulfilling and self-indulgent. She took a sip of wine and looked at me. I rested my hand on her thigh. She said, Right?

Your characteristics can explain your actions, but if there's a persuasive explanation for the source of your characteristics, I've never heard it. I once fired a lawyer who left the office every day at five. He told me he was guarding against burnout. I understand people who say they need to take care of themselves. What I don't understand is why they say it. The day I fired him, I stayed up all night working on a clemency petition for a death-row inmate I didn't represent.

When my clients ask me what I intend to do next, I don't tell them that I'll have to wait until tomorrow to figure it out, because tonight I have plans. Tonight I'm picking up a pizza and going home to play Scrabble and watch *SpongeBob* with my wife and son. When you're careening toward death, you don't want the only person who can pull the brake to look at his watch and decide it's time for lunch.

Here's what Sharon's and Tom's patients have in common with my clients: no one wants her life to depend on a stranger who might have something else, or something better, to do. I understand my clients, and I understand how the patient's reaction burdens the stranger.

■　■　■

A WEEK LATER Katya and I were having martinis at the Downing Street pub. I was smoking a Cuban cigar I had brought back with me from Mexico. Katya was eating olives. She said, Do you think Quaker did it? I told her I didn't have a clue. She said, Why would he?

I said, Same answer.

She said, I think you think he's innocent, and you don't want to say it out loud.

I said, You think you know me, don't you?

I know a lot of lawyers who want to represent a death-row

inmate who's actually innocent. Prove he's innocent, get him out, be a hero, go on TV, be adored, feel good about yourself. I understand the impulse, but I counsel them against it.

I said, You know, K, when Jeremy Winston got executed on Halloween, he was truly remorseful. I could tell that when I first met him. At some level, he felt like he deserved to die. That's why he didn't care when I told him we weren't going to win. He didn't want to win.

Winston had broken through a first-floor window and stolen Lucy Romer from her bed in the middle of the night on the Friday after Thanksgiving. Lucy's mother found her empty bed at eight the next morning. There was blood on the window frame and glass on the bed. Police found Lucy later that afternoon. She had been vaginally and anally raped. She had been smothered. Her skull was crushed, probably from being run over. She was five years old.

Winston's dad had been murdered in front of Winston when the boy was eight. Over the next seven years, his mother lived with eleven different men. At least six of them beat Winston and his mother on a fairly regular basis. One of them fired a gun at Winston. Another beat him with a brick. A third sodomized him.

Katya said, You wanted to keep Winston alive, but it wasn't your doing that he died.

I said, That rationalization hasn't worked so well for me before, and if I start to believe that he's innocent, it won't work at all with Henry Quaker.

She said, Whether you believe he's innocent has nothing to do with it.

I thought about that. I couldn't be sure whether she had

stressed the word *you* or the word *believe*. I didn't see the need to sort it out. The point was the same.

■   ■   ■

JEROME, GARY, KASSIE, AND I met to discuss our strategy. Jerome had read the transcripts. He noticed that when police arrived at the murder scene, they checked Dorris's hands for gunpowder residue. The police reports did not say what the results of the test had been. But Jerome thought it was significant that they had even conducted a test. They had to have been thinking that she killed her two children and then committed suicide. But why would they think that, why would they check her hands, unless they had found a gun nearby? And if they had found a gun nearby, why wasn't it mentioned anywhere in the file? I told the team that I'd have lunch with Detective Harmon to see what I could learn.

Gary and Kassie thought we should take another run at Green. I asked what he could possibly know. Gary had figured out from jail records that Green had been in the county jail during Quaker's trial. He could have heard just about anything. I warned them again about Green's temper. Kassie said, Right, you tell the guy to have a nice life, and *he's* the one with the temper.

I shrugged. I told Gary to let Kassie take the lead in talking to Green. Then I said to Kassie, Be sure to wear something nice.

■   ■   ■

MELISSA HARMON SAID, If you're buying lunch, you must need something.

I'd known Melissa for close to twenty years. She had been a homicide cop before leaving the police force to open her own detective agency. She is five feet two inches tall, and weighs maybe a hundred pounds after a big breakfast. She is also a third-degree black belt. For ten years she was married to an abusive spouse. I once asked her why she didn't beat the crap out of the guy. She turned her head to the side and shrugged. I never asked again. She did me a big favor when I was a young lawyer, and I was finally able to pay it back by getting her a divorce lawyer who put her ex-husband through the misery he deserved. When I needed a cop's perspective, I asked her. Sometimes I even hired her.

I said, If you were investigating a crime scene, is there any reason you would think a dead guy had committed suicide if you didn't find a gun near him? She asked what hypothetical crime scene I was talking about. I told her.

She said, Lucas Wyatt pulled that case, right? I nodded. She said, He might take too many shortcuts, but he isn't corrupt. I said that wasn't exactly what I had asked her. We were at Goode Company Bar-B-Q. She ate a piece of sausage. She said, I don't know why you eat the brisket. It's like diet food. It isn't as good as this. She stabbed another piece of sausage with her plastic fork and waved it under my nose. I waited. She said, No, I don't think that thought would cross my mind. I asked whether it would make a difference if the victim was a woman. She thought for a minute and asked, Wasn't she a mother? I told

58

her yes. She said, If the kids were dead, I might give the possibility of murder-suicide a little thought.

Even if there wasn't a gun?

If there wasn't a gun, it would be just a very little thought, she said.

I said, If Wyatt had found a gun next to the body he's not the kind of cop who would neglect to put that in his report, is he?

No, he isn't.

You sure?

She paused and said, Yeah, I am.

I said, I detected a pause before that answer.

She smiled. Then she said, I told you, he's not corrupt. If it was my time, I wouldn't waste it chasing that rabbit. But it isn't my time, is it? And if I know you, you're going to do what you're going to do. She wiped her mouth and stood up to go. Thanks for lunch, Doc. Let's do it again when I can bring more clarity to your life.

■　　■　　■

LINCOLN CALLED ME as I was driving back to the office. He had learned to ride his bike without training wheels two weeks earlier, and ever since all he wanted to do was practice. He would wake up with me at five and wait for it to get light, then ride up and down the driveway in his pajamas until it was time for breakfast. He asked whether I could come home for a while to help him practice. I told him to practice with Nana. He said,

But she runs too slow. She won't be able to help catch me if I fall. I told him that he would have to work it out. He said, You told me this morning you would practice with me at lunch. He was correct. I had forgotten. I said that something had come up at my office, and that I would have to do it tomorrow. He said, Okay, Dada. He waited for me to break the connection.

Why is it that when my six-year-old son says, *Okay, Dada*, I feel like my entire life is a waste of time?

■   ■   ■

JEROME AND BUD LOMAX were waiting for me when I got back to the office. Jerome looked at me over Bud's shoulder and rolled his eyes.

Bud Lomax was Henry Quaker's brother-in-law, Dorris's younger brother. Bud had been seventeen when Dorris and the children were killed. At Henry's trial, Lomax had testified that Dorris told him that Henry was abusive. I could not conceive of how a jury could have believed him. His eyes flitted like a bird eyeing a cat. He was a loser, and I could not imagine how anyone could believe that Dorris told him a meaningful thing. He said that Dorris was scared of Henry and once told him that Henry had threatened to kill her. Henry's lawyer did not ask him a single question on cross-examination. Three months ago he called our office, talked to Jerome, and said he needed to see us. He told Jerome that he had lied at the trial.

Jerome drove out to Bud's apartment. Bud told Jerome that

the day after the bodies were found, a detective had come to see him and said that Henry committed the crime. He said it would help if Bud could remember fights he had witnessed between Henry and Dorris. Bud said he couldn't remember any fights. He said Henry and Dorris loved each other. The detective told him it sure would be a shame if Henry got away with murdering his sister just because Bud had a bad memory. The detective came to see Bud four or five times. Eventually, his memory improved.

In the scheme of things, neither Bud's original testimony nor his recantation was of great importance. Motive is overrated as an element of criminal trials. People kill for good reasons, bad reasons, and no reason at all. But in this case, the evidence against Henry was so slim that anything helped.

Bud had served twenty months in prison for drug possession. He was twenty-seven, no longer a kid, when he called Jerome. That day in my office he smelled like he'd bathed in peppermint schnapps. I said, Happy hour started a little early today, huh, partner? He looked at me blankly. Jerome asked him to tell us again what had happened after the murder. He repeated the same story Jerome had already heard. I asked him, Where were these conversations? He said at his house. I said, Inside or outside? He said he couldn't remember. I asked him whether the detective might have found drugs inside the house. He stared at me like I had horns, with equal parts fear and disbelief. I said, How early in the morning do I need to schedule a meeting with you if I want to see you sober? He ran his thumb across his bottom lip. I told Jerome to take him home.

Later that day Jerome said, Just because the cop found drugs doesn't mean that Bud would lie, and even if we could prove he did, just because Bud lied doesn't mean Henry didn't do it.

That's true, I said. I asked Jerome whether Bud had any kids. He said, Four. Three sons, one daughter, three different mothers.

I said, Fatherhood can have unpredictable effects. I'll see you tomorrow.

■   ■   ■

I DROVE HOME to pick up Lincoln for t-ball practice. He was waiting for me, throwing a tennis ball against the garage and catching the rebound. He seemed to have forgotten about the shitty dad episode, another great thing about six-year-olds. He said, Look, Dada. Nana helped me fix my injury. He had skinned his knee falling off the bike, Maria explained, and he had insisted he needed Neosporin and an Ace bandage. He had his leg wrapped, from ankle to thigh, with an elastic bandage. I thanked Maria and told her she could go. She said to Lincoln, Adios, amor.

He hugged her and said, Hasta mañana, Nana.

Katya had wanted Lincoln to play baseball because his three best friends from school were going to. When Lincoln said he wasn't interested, I smiled. I've had enough of Little League Baseball for one lifetime. He said, I want to learn how to wrestle instead, like Dada. I thought that was a great idea. Katya gave me her be-quiet-a-minute look and asked him, Won't you be sad if all your friends are playing and you aren't?

Lincoln said, Maybe. He thought for a moment then said, Okay, I'll play if Dada will be coach. Katya gave me her gotcha look. Thus it was that I became a Little League manager, outmaneuvered by the two of them for neither the first nor the last time.

The parents in our neighborhood take Little League more than a little too seriously. They sign a contract agreeing not to abuse the umpires. Some start with the abuse anyway, and they get banned from attending the games. One banned parent sued the league, claiming he had a right to free speech, which meant he could heckle any umpire he wanted. The league hired professional coaches to train the kids. At our first practice, the professional coaches had the kids line up and told them to run to a spot on the field. Most of the kids were five; a few were six. The coach said, When you get there, break down, box-step, and throw. Eleven kids looked at me. Lincoln said, Dada, what does that mean? I told him I wasn't sure. He picked up a stick and started to draw a picture in the dirt.

The coaches were teaching the kids how to run past first base. I was still thinking about Bud Lomax. Lincoln said, Dada, I'm hot. I told him I was hot, too; just pay attention to the coaches. Sam was running to first base and crashed into Connor, who had wandered into the base path. Connor started shrieking when he saw his nose was bleeding. I wrapped some ice in a towel and pressed it against his nose. Lincoln came trotting over. I told him to go back to the other kids, that I was busy.

He said, But I'm too hot.

That's it, amigo. I'm tired of your arguing with me. We're not having a snow cone after practice.

This was a severe punishment. Snow cones are one of his favorite things to eat, and he had been talking since breakfast the day before about the flavor he was going to get. On the way to the car Lincoln pleaded with me to change my mind. When I didn't, he cried all the way home. We walked in the house and Katya asked what was the matter. I said, Sometimes I am easily the world's worst dad.

I went out back and jumped in the pool. I blew out my breath and felt myself sink to the bottom. I rolled onto my back and looked up. The sun was low in the west, casting a dancing shadow from our curly willow over the water. The shimmering surface calmed me.

Earlier that summer, a girl who had been in Lincoln's preschool class drowned at a classmate's fifth birthday party at a neighborhood country club in full view of her supposed protectors. I have heard that drowning is not a painful death, but I don't believe it. Twenty kids were swimming, and neither lifeguard saw her go under. Her hair got caught in the drain. They emptied the pool and sent the children inside and tried to revive her for half an hour before another parent who is a doctor mercifully declared her dead.

She had been an only child. I told Katya that if it had happened to Lincoln, I didn't think I'd be able to go on. Her eyes filled and she said, I know, me neither.

Under the water, I tried to imagine what the girl's parents felt, how they got out of bed in the morning. If you have other kids, you have to. If you don't, you don't. I was dizzy. I felt hollow, like the pressure had shrunk my organs and my body contained nothing but space. I sliced to the surface. When I came up, Lincoln and Winona were chasing each other around the yard. He was laughing. Her tongue was lolling to the side. She was running sawtooth slow, so he could catch her. I said, Hey Linco, you want me to go back to the field and buy you a snow cone?

He said, Nah, I think I'll just have some ice cream instead. Two scoops, one coconut crunch and one of chocolate, and a cone on the side. He paused a beat, then added, Please.

I said, I love you, amigo.

He said, I know.

■　■　■

WHILE KATYA AND I were having dinner, Kassie called. Green had been friendly. He told her that he knew for a fact that Henry was innocent. He said he knew who the killer was, and that the killing had been drug related. The killer's name was Ruben. Green told Kassie that he had been in the county jail with this Ruben during Quaker's trial. Kassie asked why he had been in jail, and Green said he'd violated his parole. She asked why Ruben was there. Green said he didn't know. She asked for Ruben's last name. Green said he forgot. Kassie hadn't pressed him for details, she just let him ramble. Kassie's major strength as a lawyer is her instinct about people who are generally untrustworthy. She said, He might have been yanking my chain, or he might not have been. It's hard to say. I'll need some time to poke around. She told me she was going to investigate the drug angle, see whether Sandra Blue, the neighbor, could remember anything helpful. I told her that sounded fine, and that she should get Gary to help her. I asked her whether there was anything else. She said, Yeah. The guy asked me if I know any recipes for soul food that he can cook on his hot plate. And one other thing, too. He masturbated while he was talking to me. Didn't try to hide it in the slightest. He's a piece of work, Doc. I'd rather not have to go see him again.

I told Katya what Kassie had said. She said, See. You should listen to me more often. I said I'd reserve judgment on that until we could figure out whether anything Green said was true. I told her about the masturbation. She said, All I'm saying is that he's actually trying to help you. Just because people are screwed up doesn't mean that nothing they say is right.

Later that night we were sitting in the library reading. I started to think about Jeremy Winston's children. I'd seen them at the prison the day I met Winston. I had given them my cell phone number, and they called me twenty times or more in less than a week. His sons were twelve and fifteen when he died. I wondered whether they went trick-or-treating on the anniversary of their dad's execution. What happens to children whose father is a murderer? I should know the answer to this question, but I don't. Nearly all my clients had terrible fathers, but only one, so far as I know, had a dad who killed someone. Isn't that curious? Lincoln wants to be a wrestler because I was a wrestler, yet my clients come to murder on their own. But what about their children? What will they tell people about their dads? How do their teachers treat them? Are their classmates scared of them?

How far into a relationship do you have to be before you tell your girlfriend that the state executed your old man?

I meet many of the parents, though I can't truly say that I know them. I wonder whether they blame themselves. I remember news footage of Timothy McVeigh's dad, in his small yard, on a riding mower, refusing to hide from the cameras. I felt like he was trying to say, I didn't kill anyone. Now let me mow my grass in peace. During a death-penalty trial, when a murderer's mother gets on the witness stand to plead with jurors to spare her son's life, the prosecutor tears into her as if she herself committed a crime, throwing in her face every bad thing her son has ever done, insinuating that she is somehow to blame. Does the prosecutor hate his own mother, or does he not see this other mother as like his own?

I'm pensive only when I have time on my hands. Socrates had it backward. He thought the unexamined life is not worth living. I think no one's life holds up to examination. The more time you spend thinking, the more you notice that everyone else is doing something better, or more important, than you. *Idleness* and *idolatry* aren't related, but they ought to be.

Winston's father was a devout Jehovah's Witness. He had forced Winston to knock on doors and invite himself in to people's homes to discuss the Bible. When Winston misbehaved, his father beat him with a tree branch or an extension cord. He didn't think he was being cruel. He thought he was being stern. He and Winston's mother got divorced when Winston was fourteen. The father moved to Louisiana. He never talked to the son again. Days before the execution, he called me to say that he believed he had been too tough on his son and to ask if there was some way he could help. He asked whether he could see his son in prison. I told him no, he couldn't. He said, I do understand. Thank you, sir. If you think it is appropriate, please tell Jeremy that I love him.

When I called Winston shortly before he died, I told him what his dad had said. If you can feel an emotion through the phone, I would swear I felt him smile, not a happy smile, more a smile of relief—no, of release, which is different, the smile of a weight being lifted.

Lincoln started to cry. I ran upstairs to his room. I tried to wake him but he was deep into a dream. He was saying, Stop, turn off, stop. I lifted him out of his bed and turned on the light. He kept screaming. I sat down at the electric keyboard in his room with him on my lap. I played two bars of Thelonious Monk's Everything Happens to Me. At last Lincoln woke up. He told me his bad dream. He had been in our exercise room and the treadmill turned itself on. The belt was whirring and the platform raised itself to the steepest incline. Lincoln pulled the plug out of the wall, but it kept on running. He said, I tried to make it stop, Dada, but it wouldn't. I told him it was okay, that it was over now. I put him back in his bed and stayed with him, stroking his damp hair, until he fell back asleep.

Katya had been standing in the hall outside his door, ready to come in and help if I needed her. When Lincoln was three and four, he had these nightmares once or twice a week. Katya used to be the only one of us who could calm him down. I would try and fail, and she would have to intervene. This night was the first time in several months that he'd had one, and I felt absurdly happy that Katya had let me handle it by myself. I made it through the day without being a total failure. I walked out of his room, feeling serene. Katya was waiting there, right outside the door. She kissed me softly and said, You're a great dad.

She always knows exactly which lie to tell.

■   ■   ■

WHEN I GOT TO THE OFFICE the next morning Kassie and Gary were already there, doing computer searches for the guy Green said had murdered Henry Quaker's family. Green had been in the jail during the Quaker trial. During two days of the trial, there was also an inmate named Ruben Francisco Cantu, the only Ruben in the jail at the same time Green was there. He'd been stopped in a routine traffic stop and when cops opened the trunk they found bricks of marijuana. He bonded out two days later. I said, So I guess the rabbit chase goes on for a little while longer, huh? I asked where Cantu was now. Kassie told me that he'd served three years of a ten-year sentence and had gotten paroled five years ago. The address we had for him was two years old, but it was all we had. I said, I think I'll take a drive over to the east side.

When the dry wind blows in from the west, carrying the petrochemical fumes toward Lafayette, the only toxic clue is that the setting sun looks like a blood orange sinking into the Sabine. People who live with poisoned air get to see the most beautiful sunsets, the bargain for not getting to see as many of them. Cantu lived five doors down from an eggshell-colored clapboard church sitting on top of cinder blocks with a listing portable sign that said, Jesus Cristo es el Hombre. I parked at the church and walked across the oyster-shell parking lot to see if anyone was inside. A man sat at a piano, picking out a tune with his left hand and jotting down the notes with his right. I said, Perdon, senor. Yo quiero saber si usted conoce a uno de sus vecinos, un hombre se llama Ruben Cantu? He asked me in English whether I was a police officer. I told him I wasn't. He said he had a lot of neighbors named Cantu. He didn't think he knew anyone named Ruben. I asked him whether I could leave my car in his parking lot, and when he said I could, I said, Muchisimas gracias, and walked down the street.

The house I hoped was Cantu's looked like a sharecropper's cabin. It had peeling white paint and a shattered window. From inside I could hear Spanish television and canned laughter. I knocked and a man wearing jockey shorts and a hooded sweatshirt opened the door. I introduced myself and said, Yo quiero hacerle unas preguntas. Usted preferie que hablar en Ingles or Espanol? My plan was to go ahead and assume he was Cantu until he corrected me.

He said, You talk Spanish like the Unabomber writes. I speak English. What do you want?

He didn't invite me in. I asked him whether he knew someone named Henry Quaker. He said no. I told him that someone I knew on death row told me he had some information that might help my client. I asked whether he knew why someone might say that. He said no. I asked whether he knew Ezekiel Green. He said no, but he delayed a brief second, and his eyes changed. He knew him. I asked whether he knew who had killed Quaker's family. He said, I already told the other guy I don't know nothing about it. That was a slip. Green's name had rattled him. As soon as he said it, he wished he hadn't. I bluffed and asked him what was the detective's name. He cocked his head to the side and didn't answer, but I knew. Some cop had talked to him. I asked him how long they had talked. He narrowed his eyes and looked at me like he was trying to figure out whether I was actually stupid or just pretending. He said, How long? Are you loco? I don't remember, man, it was a long time ago. He relaxed again, no longer nervous. I asked like how long. Days? Weeks? Months? He said, Nah, I'm talking about years ago, right after your client killed his family.

I said, A detective asked you these questions years ago?

He said, What's the matter? You don't hear so good? While I was thinking of what else to ask, he said, Adios, abogado, and he closed the door. I stood there awhile and thought about knocking, but he probably wouldn't have answered, and besides, I couldn't think of anything else to ask. So I bought a lemon aqua fresca at a taco cart that had set up in the church parking lot and headed back to town.

On the drive back I called the office and told Jerome to file a new appeal. I thought we had learned enough to entitle us to a hearing in state court. We had Green saying he knew Cantu committed the crime, and we had Cantu saying that he had been interrogated, and we had Lomax recanting and saying he incriminated Henry because a police officer pressured him to. It wasn't much, but it was something, and even though it didn't answer very many questions, it raised quite a few, which was all I could realistically hope to do at that point. It seemed likely that the cops talked to Cantu around the time of the crime, and that detail should have been in the police reports, and therefore known to Quaker's trial lawyers, but it must not have been, or Quaker's lawyer, bad as he was, would have at least talked to him. We had police testing Dorris's hands for gunpowder residue, but also no mention of a gun in police reports. Lots of dogs weren't barking. There were several threads in the case that Quaker's trial lawyer had ignored, and we needed to pull on them to see what unraveled. But the first thing I needed to do was have another conversation with Henry.

■ ■ ■

I WAS MEETING KATYA for dinner at La Griglia, and I got there a few minutes early. I ordered a martini at the bar. Jocelyn Truesdale was sitting at the end of the counter. She motioned me over. She said, You drinking alone, counselor?

I said, Hi, Judge. I'm waiting for my wife.

She said, Have I met her? The answer was no, but I did not want to be talking to Judge Truesdale about my wife. She caught the bartender's eye and pointed at her empty glass. She said, Want to buy me a drink?

I didn't. I said, Sure.

She said, I hear rumors you are going to ask me to reopen the Quaker case. Is that true? When she said *rumors* she pronounced it *rur-mors.*

I tried to think of some way that this conversation was not

highly inappropriate. I lied and said, We haven't decided what we are going to do. We might ask for a new hearing.

She said, I remember that case. It's always bothered me a little. She was drinking scotch on ice. She took a swallow and chewed a piece of ice.

Katya arrived. She saw me and took a step toward the bar. I stood up before she could walk over. I said, I'll let you know, though. I've got to go. It's been nice talking to you, Judge. I practically jogged toward Katya and steered her to our table. She asked me whom I had been talking to. I said, The judge in the Quaker case. I might need an expert opinion here, but I think she might have been coming on to me.

After we ordered, I told Katya about my conversation. She said, It's possible she was hitting on you, but she might have just been drunk. Your track record of accurately perceiving women, frankly, isn't all that great.

I told Katya the story: Truesdale had been married to a cop. She sold real estate by day and went to law school at night. Early one morning her husband pulled over a driver for drunk driving. He asked the driver to get out of the car. He didn't know it, but the driver had just robbed a gas station. The driver came out firing. Truesdale's husband was hit twice in the chest and once in the head. He died at the scene. The driver jumped back into the car and sped off. Police tracked him down the next day, but there was no video of the stop, and they couldn't find the gun. So they did what cops sometimes do when another cop gets killed. They beat the guy until he told them where he had thrown it. They found the gun in the bayou, just where he said it would be.

The case got assigned to Judge Dan Steele. Steele was a former marine. He served two tours in Vietnam before he went to law school. His law-and-order credentials were like early Clint Eastwood. But he had integrity. He ruled that the only reason the police found the gun was because they had beaten the suspect. So he concluded that the prosecutor couldn't use the gun as evidence. Without the gun, there was no case. The shooter walked. Everybody was livid, especially the victims'-rights crowd. They made it their mission to defeat Steele in the next election, and they convinced Truesdale to run against him. She crushed him. Six months after she took the bar exam, she was a criminal court judge.

I said to Katya, There is no way this case has bothered her. Nothing bothers her. We once proved that a guy who had been convicted of rape in her court couldn't have committed the crime, because the DNA didn't match. You know that she said? She said, Maybe he did it and used a condom. She figures that even if the guy didn't do what he was convicted of, he probably did something. There's not a sympathetic bone in her body. I don't buy it.

Katya said, You don't know how you would react if I got murdered. You might think you do, but you don't. Maybe her nephew is a delinquent. Maybe she found dope in her kids' clothes. Maybe she found religion. Maybe she read a good book. Maybe she started listening to Bob Dylan. Maybe she had a dream. Maybe she just spent some time meditating. Maybe she finally met someone else. Who knows? But people do change their minds, you know. I bet it really did bother her. It's a strange case.

Our food arrived. I waited until the waiter had left, then I said, Well. I still think she was just hitting on me.

Katya smiled. She said, The ego on you.

■   ■   ■

QUAKER WAS ALREADY in the cage when I got to the prison. He was eating a ham sandwich and a bag of tortilla chips. I asked him where he got the food. I was assuming he must have had a visitor I didn't know about. He said, Nicole got it for me.

Nicole is a guard on death row. She's notoriously tough. I didn't think Quaker meant her. I said, Nicole the guard?

He said, Uh-huh. I looked at him. He said, She ain't that bad. Got a tough reputation, that's all. But you act right, she treats you right. I asked whether she buys him food very often. He said, Only when I ask her. I don't ask too often. This is maybe the third time. I give her the money from my commissary; it ain't like it's her treat. I asked him whether there was anything he wanted to talk about. He said, Not really. You wanted to see me, right? He was in a sour mood. As someone who is in sour moods quite a lot, I am expert at recognizing them. Of course, he had a better excuse than I ever do. He lived twenty-three hours a day in a sixty-square-foot cell that had a cot and a stainless-steel toilet and a strip of clouded Plexiglas for a window. Guards passed him his meals through a slot in the solid-steel door. Breakfast at four, lunch at ten thirty, dinner at four. He had no television. His radio got two stations—a country

75

music station in Huntsville and a Christian talk station in Livingston. For one hour a day, guards moved him from his cell into the so-called day area, a ten-by-ten-foot caged area where he got to exercise by himself, while another inmate exercised in an adjacent cage.

People think death-row inmates have it great, that they lift weights all morning and watch TV all night, with three square meals a day, access to computers and books, and an endless series of appeals. I'm not sure whether the people who constructed this myth are ignorant, or just cynical. Either way, it's wrong in every respect. Death row is a cage at the pound. You might not have any problem with that. You might say that someone who kills someone should be kept in a cage. I don't agree with that viewpoint, but I do understand it. One day we can have the debate where I take the position that a great nation built upon the rule of law ought not to treat prisoners the way the Iranians or the Chinese do. But that wasn't the topic that day with Quaker. Instead, I needed to remember that at some point in the small remainder of every inmate's life, the exterior cage becomes interior, too. Once that happens, your client reacts to stimuli that you cannot see. It's like watching a musical without the sound. So much seems inappropriate, or inexplicable, and that makes me mad—well, not mad, exactly; *impatient* might be a better word.

I asked him whether he knew Ruben Cantu. He said he didn't. I told him what Green had told us and about my conversation with Cantu. He said, I know Green. I wouldn't believe a word he says. Anyway, I'm no lawyer, but it sounds to me like you don't have that much, just a bunch of questions, not much else. I told him I agreed with him. He said, They kill dudes in here every day who have a hundred questions. A thousand, maybe.

I couldn't argue with him about that. I said, Was Dorris depressed?

He didn't answer right away. After a moment he said, If you were married to a guy who had secrets he couldn't share and woke up every night drenched with sweat and sat around like a zombie and pushed you away when you tried to help, wouldn't you be depressed?

I said, Was she depressed enough to kill herself?

He shook his head violently. He leaned toward me. He said, She'd light herself on fire before she'd hurt those kids. I nodded.

He said, I got no interest in trying to help myself by making Dorris look bad, you understand what I'm saying? I told him I did. He said, A bunch of questions don't prove that I'm innocent.

He dropped his eyes, looking at his fingers. He was strumming them on the table, like he was playing the piano. His face softened and his eyes got wet. I had this thought: I do not want to like this man. He said, I don't know how you do what you do. Do you ever sleep?

I thought, My client Johnny Martinez asked me that very question. I said, What tune were you playing there?

Quaker played piano for the church from the time he was eight years old until the fire where he worked. On one of our earlier visits he had said to me, I ain't too religious, but I do love the music. He smiled and his eyes lit up. I told him he reminded me a little bit of Bud Powell. He said, Yeah, Dorris told me that. And I talk to myself when I'm playin', too, just like ole Bud.

He strummed his fingers some more. He said, I miss having a piano. I used to sleep good in here. It's always noisy, but I slept okay, ten or eleven hours. Lately I ain't been sleepin' at all. I don't know what's wrong with me. I filled out a form to get some medicine, something to knock me out. I nodded. From nowhere he smiled. He said, You don't seem too interested in my problems.

I said, Most of your problems I can't do anything about.

He said, I know. That's okay.

I thought of a Zbigniew Herbert poem I'd been reading: *I imagined your fingers / had faith in your eyes / the unstrung instrument / the arms without hands.*

And many verses later: *heroes did not return from the expedition / there were no heroes / the unworthy survived.*

I said, I might not be able to do anything about any of your problems, but we have raised a lot of questions, and I think we can maybe get a stay.

It was the first time I had used the word *stay*, and it was electric, an acknowledgment of the proximity of death. No stay meant Quaker would die in a few weeks. A stay meant he would survive to fight on. Survive, not thrive. Someone who thrives looks forward to tomorrow. Tomorrow for someone who only survives is just one day closer to the end.

I think all the time about what I would do if I knew how many weeks, how many days, how many hours I had left. I'd circle the date on a calendar. That's all I know. Everything else is a question. Would I sleep a lot, or not at all? Would I eat a lot, or would I have no appetite? If I ate, would I eat new foods I'd never tried, or gorge myself on my favorites? Would I watch TV or movies? Would I read books? Would I be able to concentrate? Would I exercise? What would be the point? Would I travel? Would I jump out of an airplane again, kayak huge white water, fly a jet? Would I call everyone I know and say good-bye? Would I spend every waking moment with my family, the people I love the most, or would that be too painful to withstand?

Doesn't everybody think about these things?

I didn't want Quaker not to think about these things. I didn't want to give him hope. Like I said before, I'm always hopeful, but never optimistic.

Most of my clients nod their heads at that point. Some just bow their heads. They perceive my hope like a vanishing scent. They breathe it in and memorize its smell. They cling to it when they visit their parents or their children, because it is the only reason they have to think they will visit again. They don't want to give me a chance to say anything else, anything else that might reveal how slender the reed happens to be. Not Quaker. He said, Why?

I didn't answer right away. I thought to myself, Katya is right. A sliver of belief had crept into my head and I couldn't stamp it out. It was like the aroma of baking bread. How could twelve jurors have looked at him and seen a killer? I said, Because none of this adds up.

He said, In case you're wondering, I didn't kill my family.

I almost said, *I know*, but I was not ready to surrender. I nodded.

He said, I don't know what happened to that gun, I really don't.

I wanted to nod again. I wanted to straddle the line. I wanted to support him and to protect myself. He exhaled through his nose.

I said, I know. I know you didn't.

Instantly his eyes filled with tears. His lips parted then closed. He covered his mouth and nose with his left hand. He lowered his head and lifted it. My heart was so loud I could hear it. I thought, Where do we go from here?

I said, The plan is to get some judge to believe that, too.

I wanted to run out of there. I stood up. He said, Thank you. Thank you. We touched our hands to the glass between us.

Nicole was the guard operating the electronic door that day. She asked me how my Thanksgiving had been, and I wished her a merry Christmas. I told her I'd see her after the first of the year. She said, Quaker's all right. He never causes no trouble. If you need any kind of statements from me or anyone else, you tell me, okay? There's lots of guys in here who want to help him.

I emerged from death row onto the asphalt yard at two in the afternoon. I don't believe in omens, but that didn't change the fact that the sky was turning from ochre to black. I smelled sulfur in the air. I started to hurry across the prison yard, wanting to beat the rain to my truck. Maybe the guard didn't want me to make it. While I was waiting for him to buzz me through the third of three gates, rain drops as fat as grapes began to fall. The sky crackled with lightning. Thunder like a sonic boom made me think of the night that Tim Robbins escaped from Shawshank. By the time I reached my truck, I was shivering hard and so soaked I squeaked.

■ ■ ■

THAT NIGHT I had a dream. I was driving home from seeing Quaker, down the twisting two-lane farm road that slices through fecund farmland just north of death row. The rain was pouring down, and the creek that runs along the east side of the prison was rising fast. Across from Florida's restaurant the road doglegs to the left. A canoe usually tied up at the dock behind the restaurant floated into the road. I swerved to miss it and my truck skidded into the creek. It bobbed like a cork, then pointed nosedown and started to sink. Water began to leak into the cab. I took off my seat belt and fell against the windshield. Legal papers and CDs were sliding all around me. I reached for a rock hammer I keep in my truck for just this emergency, but of course it wasn't there. Muddy water was two-thirds of the way up the door. I found the hammer and I swung it at the driver's-side window. It shattered and looked like a spider web. Instead of swinging again, I used my fist. Shards of glass pierced my wrist like a bracelet. I squeezed through the window and breaststroked upward, following the bubbles as I exhaled. I ran out of air and sucked down a greedy breath a moment too soon, so when I broke through the surface a moment later I was gagging. The rain had stopped. The sun was shining in a cloudless sky. A young boy wearing overalls and rubber boots was standing ankle-deep on the side of the creek fishing with a bamboo pole. He looked at me with no surprise and said, Hey mister, what are you doing?

■   ■   ■

THERE IS A MOMENT in the middle of every night when I am the only man alive. I slip out of bed and put on a sweatshirt. I fill a mug with hot water and a squeeze of lemon. I carry it into Lincoln's room and watch him sleep. If he's still enough, I touch his hair or stroke his cheek. I picture him and Katya sitting at the piano playing four-handed, or the two of them dancing at a wedding. Every New Year's Day, they go swimming together in the ocean. I don't need to stay alive. I've done my job. I sit at my desk and think of nothing. With headphones I listen to Art Tatum or Teddy Wilson. I wait. Sometimes I fall asleep there. Sometimes I just sit. Sometimes something comes to me. That night it was the blood. The blood might tell us something.

I crawled back into bed. Katya asked if everything was okay. I said, No, not really.

She said, It will be. She put her right leg over mine and dropped her arm over my shoulder, and for the few moments before I fell back asleep, she was right.

■ ■ ■

ON SOME DAYS, it is hard to believe that mind readers are confidence men. When I got to the office the next morning, everyone was already in the conference room. A time line and a dozen photographs of the crime scene were tacked to the wall. I went and got my rubber ball and came back. The two children had been killed in their beds. Dorris had been killed on the couch in the living room, lying on her back, a single gunshot wound in her temple. There was a trail of blood connecting the two rooms. To my eye, the drops looked thinner on the side closer to the kids, and fatter on the side closer to Dorris. That would mean that the kids died first, and the killer then walked back toward Dorris, dripping blood as he went, either from the gun or maybe from his body. Of course, your eyes often see what you want them to. Plus, the blood could have been there already, since before the murders, but there's no point to believing in coincidences, especially when they're not helpful. We had to assume that the killer trailed it from one victim to the next. But if the kids were shot first, Dorris would have heard the shots, and if she had, she would have gotten up. But she didn't get up; she was killed lying on the couch, with no signs of struggle. Nobody sleeps that deeply. That meant she had to have been killed first, probably while she was sleeping. If she was, the blood drops would be from her. If the blood wasn't from her, if it was from one of the children, then maybe she did commit suicide after all, first shooting her kids and then taking her life. The story was in the blood. We needed to test the blood drops and see who they came from and to see which direction the killer was walking.

I asked Gary, our in-house chemist, to write a motion asking the judge to let us test the blood and then to arrange for a lab to test it. Jerome was going to arrange to have Quaker polygraphed. The results of the test would not be admissible in a court proceeding, but if we got down to the eleventh hour and had to ask the governor to intervene, it would help to be able to say that Quaker had passed the lie detector. You might as well ask a Magic 8 Ball for advice, but if the governor believed in the wizard, I wasn't going to pull back the curtain.

Gary and Kassie were going to line up the witnesses for the trial. We would bring in Green from death row to testify about what he had heard, and Bud, Dorris's brother, would say that he had lied at the trial. We'd get Detective Wyatt to say that he had tested Dorris's hands for gunpowder residue, and we might walk blind into an alley and ask him why he tested her hands. We would try to make sure Ruben Cantu was there, to say detectives had interviewed him, but I had a feeling Cantu was going to be hard to find again. It wasn't nearly enough to prove that Quaker was innocent, but our goal wasn't to prove that he was innocent. The goal was to create a little mayhem to buy more time. If we could keep him alive, we could try to figure out what had really happened. If we could figure out what really happened, we could keep him alive.

I went outside to walk around the block. There was nothing for me to do but wait. I walked by the cloisters. Two men sitting next to one another on a bench by a fountain looked so serene I thought they were fake, until they nodded to me in unison. Last fall I had taken a weeklong course on Buddhist meditation. The room smelled like sweaty feet, and when I tried to clear my mind, it would fill with images of lavender virus cells under a microscope. I should have spent the time working on another case, but when you cannot help but believe that an innocent man's life is in your care, it can prove difficult to divert your attention to another pressing task.

My cell phone rang. It was Judge Truesdale. I stopped in midstride and stepped closer to a building. I looked behind me. It felt like someone was watching. She said, I just signed an order granting you a hearing in the Quaker case.

I had forgotten we even filed a request for a hearing. We always ask, and they are never granted. I thought, How did she get my cell phone number? Then I realized, She had probably called the office first and gotten it from someone there.

I said, Thank you, Judge.

She said, You are welcome, Professor. I told you this case bothered me.

She told me that we were set for the last week of January, and I told her I would see her then. She said, If not before.

When I got back, everyone was still in the conference room eating donuts. I put my phone down on the table and gave it a spin, like I was playing spin-the-bottle. I told the team we had a hearing in less than five weeks. Kassie asked, How do you know that? I told them that Judge Truesdale had called me. Kassie said, She called you on your cell phone to say she had signed an order?

There is little distance between calmness and irresponsibility. I am no Zen master, but I live far from the edge. When the plane is crashing, I will be as scared as everyone else, but I will be the one who isn't screaming.

I said, Which one of you gave her my cell phone number? Gary stuffed half a cake donut into his mouth. Kassie stared at me. I looked at Gary and said, Was it you?

He swallowed and said, Are you kidding?

I said, Well, she got it from somebody.

Jerome said, That's pretty weird.

I said, I think she might actually be bothered by the case.

Kassie said, Right.

I reached for a glazed donut and took a bite, and I felt happy. It was three days before Christmas. We had an execution date in six weeks and a hearing in five, not a lot of time. I said, Tick tock, folks.

■　■　■

QUAKER'S ONLY LIVING blood relative was his mother, Evelina. Quaker was the younger of two boys. His older brother Herbert died of a heroin overdose when Quaker was eight. Quaker found Herbert lying on the floor of the bedroom they shared, a tourniquet around his biceps, a needle hanging out of his arm. He dialed the operator and said his brother was asleep and wouldn't wake up. EMT workers found him next to the body, saying, Open your eyes, Herbie. Please open your eyes.

Evelina had heard the news that we were going to have a hearing. She called me. She said, I apologize for bothering you, sir. I know you are a busy man. I told her that she wasn't bothering me. She said, I need to do what I can to help Henry. My manager said he can give me the week off so I can come to Houston. Is that what I should do, sir? She lives in Temple, a four-hour-drive away, and works as a cashier at a grocery store. I told her she didn't need to do anything and there was no reason for her to come to Houston. I tried to explain that the hearing was going to involve technical legal issues. I promised I would call her every day to let her know how things were going. She said, You do believe that Henry is innocent, don't you, sir?

I decided to stop at the pool on the way home and go for a swim. I had an hour before Lincoln's last t-ball practice of the year. It was four o'clock. The pool was empty. I tried to count my laps, but I kept losing track. I couldn't stop the number *4* from appearing in my brain. They were scrolling across my retina on a film reel that counts down from ten until the movie begins, but every frame had the number *4*, and it didn't stop. *4, 4, 4, 4, 4.* It was in black-and-white. The color part of my brain had malfunctioned. I wondered what it would be like to see the world without color, like a dog. I realized I knew already from old TV. *Perry Mason* was black-and-white. So was *Leave It to Beaver.* Wally and the Beav. If the older brother is a delinquent, does the younger brother have a chance? Then another *4* appeared, and I lost the thread of my thought. I looked at my watch and decided to swim for twenty minutes. I proposed to Katya on February 4. She and I walked with Winona over to the park where we had had our second date, a picnic lunch. I unhooked Winona from her leash and she stood next to me, leaning against my legs, wanting to be even closer, not understanding the physical limits on proximity. Katya and I sat on a bench and I opened a bottle of champagne I had in my backpack. I told her she was the most amazing person I had ever met and would she marry me. Saying that meant more than her answer. To me, the moment was more magical even than the day we got married, because it was just us. Had I forgotten all that when we settled on the same date for Quaker's execution, or did I have some unwarranted faith that we'd survive that day?

I looked at my watch. I'd been swimming more than half an hour. I pulled myself out of the pool. My heart was racing like a newborn's. Wasn't it Rousseau who loved mankind and hated man? That's me. I do not want my clients to be executed, and I can't stand them. Why can't I help somebody who didn't kill someone?

Before I left my office that afternoon I decided we would do nothing to try to stave off the execution of Ronnie O'Neill. He'll be the first person executed after the new year—on January 12, if all goes according to the state's plan. We can't help everyone, and we're focused on Quaker.

All decisions to do nothing are hard. This one was especially so. O'Neill is mad. Murderers are often sociopaths, but most of them are not crazy. Not so with O'Neill. He heard voices telling him to kill his ex-wife. He'd been sent to a mental hospital fourteen times. When the cops came to arrest him after the murder, they knew his name. O'Neill shouted to them through the window that he would be right out and surrender himself. They waited. O'Neill took a shower, dressed himself in a suit and tie, walked out the front door, and lay facedown in the grass until the police came over and cuffed him. At the trial, the judge let O'Neill fire his lawyers and represent himself. The judge knew one thing: You don't lose any votes greasing the rails for murderers. O'Neill wore a purple cowboy outfit to court, complete with boots, chaps, and spurs. His Mexican sombrero hung from a string that circled his neck like a choker. He had a toy pistol in a holster on his hip. He issued subpoenas to Pope John Paul II, Anne Bancroft, and John F. Kennedy, Jr. He rambled like a lunatic while the judge dozed at his bench. The jury spent less than fifteen minutes deliberating before sentencing him to death. The judge appointed a new lawyer to handle the appeal. Then he let O'Neill fire that lawyer, too. O'Neill filed no appeal. He wrote a letter to the judge asking for a speedy execution date, and the judge obliged. I went to see him on death row to ask whether he wanted to reinstate his appeal. O'Neill leaned close to the window and whispered into the phone, No worries, sir. Their chemicals can't kill me. They will make me invisible and I will walk out of here. I will put you on my witness list if you would like so you can see the miracle for yourself. Jesus has arranged it all. I'll be preaching the good gospel by the coming dawn. I asked him again whether he wanted me to do something. He said, Don't you dare. Then he said, And forgive me for saying this, sir, but if you try, I will be forced to strike you mute. Heed my admonition, sir. I implore you. I thanked him for coming out to see me. He held a finger to his lips and winked at me.

Jerome is the office conscience. He asked what we were going to do for O'Neill. He was holding half a fresh baguette, the only food he would eat all day. I noticed how thin his arms are.

So that I wouldn't have to look him in the eye, I looked at the wall chart that shows the workloads of the lawyers in my office. No one has time to try to save O'Neill's life. I said, Nothing. We're not going to do anything. We don't have any more capacity, and besides, O'Neill doesn't want our help.

He opened his eyes wide and stared at me for a moment. He

looked like he was rehearsing what to say. Then he turned and walked out without saying a word.

■ ■ ■

LINCOLN WAS WAITING in the driveway for me as I pulled up to the house. I changed clothes and we got on the tandem bike and rode to practice. The professional coaches were trying to teach the kids to field grounders. Lincoln was playing second base. The coach hit him a soft ground ball, and it rolled between his legs into right field. The shortstop, Alexander, came over to Lincoln and pushed him in his chest. Lincoln said, Hey, why'd you do that? On the way home, after practice, Lincoln said, Alexander is mean. He pushed me for no reason. I told Lincoln that some kids are like that. He asked me why. I said I wasn't sure.

Here's a bet I'd be willing to wager: Alexander is going to be a bully. He's going to spend time in detention. He'll get in some fights. But he's a middle-class kid with middle-class parents living in a brick house in a nice neighborhood where people walk their dogs and kids ride their bikes in the middle of the street. He'll never murder anyone. I'd bet my life.

We stopped at the grocery store on the way home. Lincoln wanted a slice of pizza. I asked the butcher for an organic chicken, which I planned to roast with olive oil, lemon, and lots of garlic. Lincoln said, Please don't buy a chicken, Dada. When he was four, Lincoln loved chicken nuggets. One day he asked where they came from. I told him. He asked, Do they have to kill the chicken? When I told him that they did, he said, Then I'm not going to eat them anymore. It's not nice to kill little chickens. He hadn't eaten meat or fowl since. He has a Hindu friend at school. At a restaurant last week, when the waitress asked him whether he wanted a grilled cheese or a cheeseburger, he said, I have to have a grill cheese. Vijay and I are vegetarians. And I would also like some lemonade, please. And carrot cake for dessert.

When Katya was pregnant and the obstetrician told us we were going to have a boy, I knew I would love my son. Parenthood is just one cliché after another. What I didn't know was that I would admire him.

I said, Amigo, I sure do admire you. But I like meat.

He said, Well, you shouldn't. The animals didn't do anything mean to you, did they?

That night, after Lincoln went to sleep, I told Katya about my conversation with Evelina. She drank some wine and said, You can't save everyone, you know. She peeled the wishbone out from the piece of chicken she was eating. Here, she said, break this with Lincoln in the morning.

The next day, before he went to school, Lincoln and I broke the wishbone. Again he got the bigger piece. He said, Do you want to know what I wished?

I said, Sure, amigo, but you don't have to tell me if you don't want to.

He said, I know. But I don't mind. I wished that I die at the same time as you and Mama, so that way, none of us ever has to be alone.

91

I'm sure there's a good way to answer that, but I don't know precisely what it is.

■　■　■

OUR PARALEGAL BUZZED ME the next morning and told me Eze-kiel Green was on the line. Death-row inmates cannot make phone calls. They can talk with their lawyers, but only by prearrangement. I asked her whether she was sure. She said, That's what he said.

Green said, I can't talk long, but I heard about your hearing. You need to bench-warrant me up there so I can help.

A bench warrant is an order a judge signs to have an inmate transported to the courthouse. I said, How are you calling me?

He said, Cell phone, man. Don't worry, it's all cool.

I didn't want to know what kind of favors Green was trading with a guard to be able to call me on a cell phone. I said, I don't think the judge is going to hear from any witnesses. But I'll let you know. And if you call me again, I'll tell the warden.

Green said, Merry Christmas, counselor, and he broke the connection.

■　■　■

WINTER IS MY FAVORITE time at the beach. Every year, Katya and I drive down to Galveston a day or two before Christmas

92

and stay until after the first of the year. We have the beach to ourselves. We go on long walks, read, watch the waves, and drink margaritas on the deck. I was going to cancel this year, but Quaker was going to get executed anyway, so why bother?

The day before Christmas Lincoln wanted to practice riding his bike on the beach. When he hit the soft sand, his front tire started to wobble. He squeezed the front brake and went flying over the handlebars. His face hit the sand. He cut his cheek, right below his left eye, and his forehead. He bit through his lip. Blood was streaming down his face and he was crying. I told him falling is normal and he should get back on the bike. He was crying harder. When he gets older, he is going to encounter bad people. He needs to be able to defeat them, or at least avoid being hurt by them. I said, Get back on the bike, amigo, or we are going to take it back to the store. A woman walking down the beach looked at me oddly, but I was not screaming. I wasn't. Lincoln was sobbing so hard he was shaking.

Just then, Katya came running up to us, and Lincoln wrapped his arms around her. While she stroked his hair, I told her what happened. She said to me in a stage whisper, Can I walk home with him?

I said, Fine. It might have been closer to a hiss.

When O'Neill was twenty-one years old, he rode a kid's tricycle through his neighborhood. I've seen photographs. He looked like a circus clown. He wasn't doing it to be funny. He played with kids who were six years old. The neighbors thought he was simpleminded but harmless. They were half right.

I pushed Lincoln's bike for a while, then picked it up and

carried it the rest of the way home. The dog usually ran ahead of me, attacked some waves, chased some gulls, and waited for me to catch up. This day she was walking ten yards behind me, like she was embarrassed. Another hall-of-fame parenting day.

Lincoln ate some soup and went to sleep. Katya said, Do you want to go back to Houston? I told her no. She said, Okay. But Lincoln and I will understand if you change your mind. She read until she fell asleep on the couch. I carried her to bed and put Lincoln in bed next to her. I carried a bottle of bourbon out onto the deck and listened to the ocean that was too dark to see. At three I crawled into bed. At five I got up and started to work on my outline for the Quaker hearing. My phone buzzed. I had gotten a text message. It said, Quaker needs to see you. It was signed EG.

At eight I called Jerome, who is also the office ethicist, and asked him whether I needed to report Green to the warden. I was pretty sure it was illegal for death-row inmates to have access to cell phones, meaning I knew a crime was being committed. Green was not my client, so I did not have any duty of loyalty toward him. Jerome said, Don't you think we need to keep Green warm in case he really knows something about Quaker? I asked Jerome to set up a meeting for me to see Quaker on December 30. He said, One other thing. I went ahead and wrote up something for O'Neill. I'm going to e-mail it to you. I'd like to get it filed the day after Christmas, so can you look at it today?

I said, I thought we decided not to do anything for O'Neill.

Jerome said, Actually, you decided that. But you said that it was based on nobody's having time. I couldn't sleep last night so I had eight hours to write the motion. I didn't think you'd care what I did on my time.

I told him I would look at it right away.

There's nothing quite like being the boss.

■   ■   ■

For the next few days, I did not turn on my computer or check my voice mail. I was completely focused on trying to avoid being a terrible dad.

My dreams were not so forgiving. The night before I was going to drive to the prison, I dreamed that Katya, Lincoln, the dog, and I were hiking up at Guardsman Pass. It was late November. A dusting of snow covered the steel-hard ground. Deep in the forest, we drank soup from a thermos and ate saltine crackers and chocolate. When we got back to the truck I asked Katya where Lincoln had run to. She said she thought I had him. Winona was running back and forth, nose to the ground, agitated. There was less than an hour of daylight left. Katya and Winona took off to retrace our steps. Just then Henry Quaker came out of the woods, carrying Lincoln on his back. Winona started to bark, a sound of joy. Lincoln was saying, Hooray for Henry, Hooray for Henry.

Maybe we don't love our son more than you love yours, but I'm certain we love him more than my clients' parents loved theirs. Henry might have been an exception.

At dawn on the thirtieth I went for a run with the dog. When

I got back I wrote a note for Katya and Lincoln saying I'd be home in time for dinner. I drove off to see Quaker.

■ ■ ■

I TOLD QUAKER that his mom had called me. He asked whether that was why I was there on the day before New Year's Eve. I told him about the message from Green. He said, The only time I talk to the guy is to say, What's up? I didn't tell him nothing about my case.

I'd driven four hours to see a client who did not need to see me.

I asked Quaker whether he wanted anything to eat. He said, They got beer in those machines? He smiled. He said, You know, I was planning on going to see Dorris on the day the police came to get me.

I had avoided asking Quaker what had happened between him and Dorris, but I felt like I had to. It was like listening to a fairy tale. He had gone to a basketball game with her when he was in ninth grade, and that night when he got home he told his mama that he had met the woman he was going to marry. He said to me, This is corny, man, but the first time I talked to her, I felt like I'd known her forever. I knew we belonged together.

Nicole, the guard, came over. She asked Henry how he was doing. I would have sworn she winked at him. She told me Happy New Year and walked away. I looked at Quaker. He shrugged.

Quaker said, Was it love at first sight for you?

I said, I thought love was only true in fairy tales.

He said, Then for someone else but not for me. I love that song. Did you know that Neil Diamond wrote it for the Monkees?

I hadn't known that. I said, Seriously?

He said, Yeah. Some famous jazz critic, first time he heard Bill Evans, thought the guy was a lounge player. Can you imagine that? Bill Evans?

I had heard that. I said, There's a certain kind of talent that you have to learn to appreciate.

He said, The flip side of belonging together the way we did is that Dorris needed me, needed me a lot. She was one of those girls who needed to talk and talk. I didn't have to say nothing, just so long as I was listening, you know? And she liked to be touched. Holding hands, neck rubs. Didn't matter what. She wanted me to be close to her.

There was a fly buzzing around inside the cage where he was sitting. It landed on his hand. He didn't try to kill it, just shooed it away.

He said, She needed *intimacy*. He stressed the word, like maybe I didn't know what it meant.

He said, After the fire, I couldn't give her what she needed. I tried. I really did.

His eyes lost focus, like he was seeing the scene. He continued, One time I had this dream that my hands got cut off, but I didn't even know it till I sat down at the piano in church and couldn't play. I looked and they were just stubs. I felt all them people in the pews watching me. That's what it was like. I was trying, but what I needed was gone.

He did not need any reassurance from me. I don't even know

97

if he needed me to listen, but I wanted to. He told me about the morning it happened: He was fixing breakfast for Daniel and Charisse. Standing at the stove, wooden spoon in hand, he saw he was no longer what she needed. It was a vision, not a thought, and it did not come gradually, but instead overwhelmed him, suddenly, unexpectedly, and completely. He said, It reminded me of the story in the Bible about Esau, Jacob's twin brother, how he's born fully developed. It was like being in a fun house at a carnival. Nothing looked familiar. He wasn't sure which of the kids asked him to put sausage in the eggs, or whether they wanted butter on their toast.

He said, It was sort of like losing my memory, except I remembered enough to know I was losing it. Isn't that strange?

When he told her he was missing the parts that made them right for each other, Dorris said she could wait it out, wait until he was back to normal again, however long it took. But the way he was was the way he was going to be. He knew it. He fantasized about driving off into the desert, or swimming out into the ocean, and just surrendering. He said, God has a plan for us all. I was ready for Him to take me so He could take care of my family. I asked him why he hadn't. He looked at me with what I thought was surprise, but it might have been pity. He said, The kids, man. I had two kids. The Lord will provide bread, but He doesn't go to ball games or swim meets. Just 'cause I was no good for Dorris didn't mean Daniel and Charisse would be better off with no dad.

One minute I felt like we were connecting. The next I felt impossible distance. I got up to go to the bathroom. I splashed water on my face and looked in the stainless-steel mirror at the dark circles under my eyes. There was no trash can for my paper towel. I flipped it into the toilet and flushed it away. I felt an overwhelming urge to go home. When I came out an inmate I had not met was wildly waving me over. I picked up the phone. He said, You know me? I shook my head. He said, I'm Greg Whitaker. Come see me, okay? I didn't kill nobody. I was there, but I didn't pull the trigger. Can you please come see me? I told him I'd try and I put down the phone. Whitaker? I knew something about the case but I couldn't think of it. My brain felt thick.

I walked back over to Quaker. He was reading. I said, What did you tell your lawyer about the insurance?

Everything about him felt so sincere, so completely honest. I wanted him to lie to me. I wanted him to give me a reason not to believe a word he said. He said, Oh, the insurance. I wondered when you were gonna ask. That was the agent's idea. I was just planning on getting insurance for the cars. She told me that it's a good way to save money. I told Dorris about it. She said to go on ahead. We had two children. We needed to save for college. So I bought it. I kinda thought it was a waste of money, but they just took it out of my paycheck.

He said, Do you have life insurance? I told him I didn't. He said, See, that's what I'm saying. Smart dudes like you don't buy it. Why should I?

We sat silently for a while. Then he said, How come you ain't asked about the blood? I shrugged. Please, I thought, tell me a fucking lie. He said, If it was really Danny's, it must have been from one of his nosebleeds. He had 'em all the time.

It hadn't really occurred to me that the blood might not be

Daniel's. I asked him whether he had told his lawyer about the nosebleeds. He said, 'Course I did. Told the police, too.

I told him the next time I would see him would be at the hearing and asked if he needed anything in the meantime. He said, I could use some more books. I'm reading this dude named Tim O'Brien. He's got books about Vietnam. They resonate with me.

I said, Resonate?

He grinned and said, I got plenty of time in here to get educated.

I told him I'd send him some books, and I stood up to leave. He hesitated, I saw it, but then he put his hand on the glass to say good-bye.

■   ■   ■

It's NOT FASHIONABLE to believe in truth, but what can I say? There's good and bad, right and wrong, true and false. My conversation with Quaker left me dizzy. It was gray outside. The drizzle felt like pricks of ice. I hallucinated. I saw Quaker swirling in black water, his white jumpsuit like the middle of an Oreo. Have you heard of the Coriolis force? The mathematics are complicated (Google *Laplace's tidal equations* if you want to see for yourself), but that's not what I was struggling with. It was something else. Coriolis is true, but the belief that it influences which way the water spins on its way down the toilet is false. And it remains false even if a million people, a billion, think it's true. It doesn't matter which direction he was spinning. Here's what I was thinking: Either way, he's dead.

In *The Things They Carried*, Tim O'Brien says, *A thing may happen and be a total lie; another thing may not happen and be truer than the truth.* He's right, and the more important thing is that he is not disagreeing with me. A jury of middle-class white people spent a week looking at a sullen unshaved black man and listening to a passionate prosecutor while the black man's lawyer slept, and there were three dead bodies, and two of them were children, and when you see pictures of a dead child, especially one who's been shot, you *need* to know who did it, believe me you do. They believed her version: *a true story that never happened.*

But just because you believe in black-and-white doesn't mean that you can't also believe in gray, because even though something that is true cannot be a lie, and even though a lie can never be true, not everything that is true is equally true. *Happening truth* is not false; it is just less true than *story truth.*

Happening truth just *is*; story truth needs a teller. That's what law is. The facts matter, but the story matters more. The problem we faced is Quaker's story had already lost, and the only truth that mattered now was the one that I didn't have the facts to tell.

■ ■ ▨

LINCOLN'S MIDDLE NAME is Peter, after Katya's dad. Peter died from metastatic melanoma when he was sixty, a month before our second wedding anniversary. Katya's mom has never even thought of remarrying. She believes in soul mates. Her husband was her life.

I envied their relationship. Katya feared it. She didn't want her world to end if I died prematurely, or if I woke up one day and walked off to be alone with myself. She set up a page on Facebook and collected a couple hundred friends. She started competing in Latin ballroom dance.

It seemed to me like she was nurturing a parallel life in case ours ended too soon. I told her that. She said I was being ridiculous, but I noticed that she didn't deny it.

One night she and some of the dancers from her studio went out for sushi and then club-hopping. At midnight she called to say she was on the way home. The club was fifteen minutes away. Half an hour later, she still wasn't home. I called her cell phone and went straight to voice mail. I sat in the upstairs reading area of our house, a Cormac McCarthy novel open on my lap, and stared out the floor-to-ceiling windows at the street she'd have to come down. Ten minutes later I called her cell phone for the second time, and again five minutes after that, then a fourth time. At one fifteen she answered.

Where the fuck are you?

What's the matter with you? Janet lost her keys. I've been trying to help her find them.

I said, You told me you were coming home more than an hour ago.

She said, Since when do you worry about me? I thought you'd be asleep. You're always asleep when I come home late.

The truth of that observation jolted me. I said, I don't think you can draw any inferences from the fact I fall asleep early sometimes.

She said, That's true.

I tried to figure out whether I was mad or worried. I've heard that anger is never the first emotional reaction. Maybe I was worried and then mad. Or maybe jealous and then mad. If I'm going to need her, shouldn't she need me, too?

■ ■ ■

BEFORE KATYA AND I were married, while she was still practicing law, we had plans to go to her law firm's annual meeting in New York. Our flight left Friday morning. On Thursday I went to the prison to see Moises Ramirez. Ramirez was scheduled to be executed the following week. He was not our client. He had written me five letters in three days, begging for help.

When he came into the cage he was wearing horn-rimmed glasses and had peach fuzz on his chin. He looked like the character who played Michael J. Fox's father in the first *Back to the Future* movie. He had a tattoo on his left forearm that said Clara. I had no idea what he had done. I was there to tell him there was nothing I could do.

I said, I talked to your lawyers and told them I was going to come talk to you.

He said, I ain't heard nothing from my lawyers in like five years. They don't live in Texas no more, do they?

In fact, his lawyers *had* left the state. But I was surprised they

103

had not even written him. I asked, Who told you about your execution date?

First time I heard about it was when the major called me into his office. That was a month ago.

I looked down at my notebook. I wrote the word *Scared*. He said, I been writing my pen pals. Cheryl, she lives in West Virginia, wrote me back and gave me your address. I just need some kind of help, man. I want y'all to represent me. My pen pals can get y'all some money.

I said, The problem isn't money. The problem is that it is really too late to file anything else.

His lower lip quivered. I thought, Please don't start crying.

That morning the Supreme Court had decided a case having to do with the obligations of lawyers appointed to represent death-row inmates in federal court. In my office we had started constructing an argument based on the new case we thought might buy some more time for a few of our clients. I did not want to waste it on Ramirez.

I said, The Supreme Court decided a case today that we might be able to use to get you a stay.

He said, What's that?

I said, A stay means you won't get executed next week.

He said, No. I know. But then what? Does it mean I get another month or something?

I said, At this point, the only goal is to get you a stay. If you don't get executed next Wednesday, then we can try to figure out what else to do.

The phrase *blank stare* was invented to describe the look he was giving me. I could not tell whether he did not understand what I was saying, or whether he did not like what I was saying. I said, I'm not going to file anything unless you want me to.

He said, I want you to do anything you can.

I said, Okay, but let me explain how it will work before you decide that.

I went through the normal speech, telling him that we would probably lose, and that we would not know we had lost until twenty minutes before six, and that I would call him and he would not have a chance to prepare or tell anyone good-bye.

He said, I ain't got nobody I have to say good-bye.

Okay. But you still won't have much time to get ready.

So you don't think I'll get me a stay?

I said, I think there is at most a one percent chance you'll get a stay.

What's that?

What's a stay?

No. A one. What did you say?

I said there is no more than a one percent chance we'll win.

He said, Yeah, that. What is it? Like out of a hundred?

I said, Percent? Yes. It's like there are a hundred Ping-Pong balls. One chance we will win. Ninety-nine chances we will lose.

He said, Okay. Yeah. I want you to.

That night I told Katya about the visit. She knew what was coming. I said I couldn't go to New York. She said, For somebody who claims he doesn't want people depending on him you sure create a lot of dependency.

I said, I know it won't make any difference, but I think it helps him to know someone is out there trying to help him. Katya didn't say anything. I said, I think the worst thing is to feel completely alone in the universe.

Katya was mad I was not going to go to New York. She said, I get that.

■   ■   ■

LINCOLN AND KATYA were watching *SpongeBob SquarePants* when I got back to the beach. Lincoln ran over and hugged me. I pretended that he knocked me down and we rolled around on the floor, me tickling him, until he begged me to stop. Katya said, How did it go?

I said, Quaker asked me whether when I met you it was love at first sight.

She laughed. She said, Did you lie and say yes?

I said, If I had said yes it wouldn't have been a lie. It just took me several years to realize it.

She said, Right.

Lincoln said, What's love at first sight? Katya explained that it is when two people know as soon as they meet each other that they want to be with each other forever. Lincoln said, That's impossible.

Katya looked at me and smiled. She said, He's definitely your son.

■   ■   ■

On the western tip of Galveston Island, where the Gulf of Mexico meets the bay, only the ignorant stray far from shore. The vicious swirling currents pull overconfident swimmers out to the open seas and drown a dozen unsuspecting fishermen a year. I got into my kayak and floated into it. Underneath it's a maelstrom, but from on top of the water, where I intended to stay, it seemed peaceful and calm. The Buddhist river runners I used to know would say that the secret was never to fight the river. I was willing to go wherever the tides wanted to put me.

I saw a couple of dorsal fins. I thought the dolphins had come over to play, then I saw that there was only one fin, not two, and that it was a shark. It was only six feet long, which is long enough when you're floating in a plastic seven-foot boat in the middle of the ocean. A school of jellyfish, thousands of them, streamed toward my boat, then fanned out along its length, half reaching toward the bow, half toward the stern, forming a torus, and rejoining into a line on the other side. It was cold, a hard wind blowing in from the north, the second day of the new year, and at 3:00 p.m., the sun was already low in the western sky. Four pelicans flew in a line, nose to tail, not a foot above the surf. I watched them until they were a dot. Looking south toward Cuba, I saw nothing, not a boat, not a rig, not a man, just the horizon, and a sliver of moon. The tide pushed me a mile to the east, where the waves began lapping, easing me to the shore. An hour later I was aground. I laced on my shoes and jogged back up the beach, through the soft sand, to my truck. By the time I got back to our cabin, Katya and Lincoln were back from shopping, and my mind was washed. Lincoln asked whether we could go build a sand castle before dinner, and I said sure.

Katya and I sat on the deck and ate fried trout while Lincoln watched TV and ate buttered spaghetti. When I was ten, my brother Mark, who was then eight, decided to be a vegetarian. We had a housekeeper named Evelina, just like Quaker's mom. The second day of Mark's vegetarianism, she made pepper steak, his favorite, stirring thinly sliced flank steak in a cast-iron skillet with just a tad of oil, some garlic, a tablespoon of freshly ground peppercorns, and sliced jalapeños. Mark ate two servings. We shared a room. That night, as we were going to sleep, he said, If I'm going to be a vegetarian, I'm not going to be able to eat some things I really like. I told him that was true. He nodded like he had had a great insight then told me good night. He did not eat meat again for more than fifteen years.

Katya said, Where did you go? I told her I was thinking about how Henry's mom had the same name as a woman who used to cook for us. She said, I think this case is officially under your skin. I told her she might be right. We decided that she and Lincoln and the dog would come back to Galveston in a month, while I would be occupied with the Quaker hearing, so that I did not drive them crazy, and vice versa. We told Lincoln the next day on the drive back to Houston.

He said, But it won't be fun without Dada. I told him that he and Mama would have plenty of fun. He said, I know. It will still be pretty good, but not great. He spread his hands two feet apart. He said, If this is great...Then he held his hands two inches apart and said,...and if this is terrible...He held his hands about six inches apart and said, Going to Galveston without Dada will be this good. Katya leaned over and kissed him on the head. He said, Dada, I'm hungry.

We stopped for ice cream. Walking back to the truck, Lincoln noticed the tape measure next to the door. He asked why it was there. I told him that if the place got robbed, and police asked the clerk how tall the thief was, she wouldn't need to guess. Lincoln asked why someone would steal, and I said that there are some bad people in the world. He said, But maybe he just needs money to eat. I said that might be possible. Lincoln said, Besides, if he's bad, Dada, he might shoot the person. I told him that was true. He said, Remember when Mia pulled my hair? I told him yes, I did. He said, I still don't understand why some people are bad. I just don't get it.

■   ■   ■

Lincoln started getting night terrors when he was almost two. He would start to cry softly, and it would grow, crescendo-like, until he was screaming. His eyes would be closed. Katya or I would lift him from his bed, and he would be limp and tense, back and forth, eyes shut, shrieking. We would pace, turn on the lights, talk to him loudly. Minutes would go by, sometimes five, sometimes ten. He would finally stop without ever waking, and in the morning recall nothing.

I knew these terrors were not my fault, and that they were. They started the night that Julius Anthony died. Anthony lived

on death row for twenty-two years. He and two of his gang buddies shot an elderly woman for her Cadillac when Anthony
was nineteen. His friends fired the shots. Anthony only drove
the car, but the others were two years younger and not yet old
enough to be executed for the crimes, so Anthony was the only
one sentenced to die. On death row he grew up. By the time
he died, he was not remotely the same person he had been.
Six guards wrote letters, pleading with the governor to spare
his life. They said they supported the death penalty, but not
for Anthony. He was a peacekeeper, they wrote; he had intervened in fights and saved guards' lives. He had counseled other
inmates. He was not a risk to anyone and he caused others not
to be risks as well. The governor turned them down, issuing
a boilerplate statement the day of the execution that said the
jury had spoken. The chaplain told me that it took prison officials forty-five minutes of poking to get the needle inserted into
a vein. One of the guards on the tie-down team was crying.
Anthony told him not to worry, that everything would be okay,
the inmate consoling the executioner. After the execution, the
victim's son and I found ourselves standing next to one another
outside the execution chamber, a rare social blunder by prison
officials. He put his arm around me and leaned his head on my
shoulder. A reporter called me on my cell phone while I was
driving home to ask me how it felt. I told him to hold on for a
moment. I put the phone down on the passenger seat, and left
it there for the two-hour drive back to Houston.

When I got home that night Katya was sitting in the rocking
chair in Lincoln's room listening to her iPod. She stood up and
hugged me, and we watched him together, his arm wrapped

tightly around a teddy bear. We went downstairs and I poured us a drink. An hour later, Lincoln was wailing.

■　■　■

As I PULLED onto the freeway after our stop for ice cream on the drive home from Galveston, I saw a flash of lightning out of my right eye. I asked Katya whether she had seen it. She said no, and then I saw it again. A window shade came down, and just like that, the top half of my vision was gone. I said, Uh-oh. Lincoln asked me what was wrong. I told him nothing. I asked Katya to drive. She heard something in my voice and didn't ask why. When we got out of the car to change seats, I told her I couldn't see out of my right eye. I called my neighbor, an eye surgeon, and he told me to come over as soon as we got back to town.

I walked next door to Charlie's house. He looked at me and drove us to his office. He dilated my eyes and told me that my retina was torn into the macula, and he wanted to operate on me the next day. He explained that the retina is the layer across the back of the eyeball that serves as the film for the eye. Images go from the retina to the optic nerve to the brain. I needed to have the retina repaired, or I would be blind. He said, I told you to stop boxing. I reminded him I had quit sparring more than ten years earlier. He said, Hmmm.

I asked about the recovery time and Charlie said I would not be able to do any work for a week, maybe two, perhaps as long as three. I told him there was no way I could put things off for

111

that long. He said, The alternative is that you go blind. I asked him what were the percentages of that. He said, Of going blind with an unrepaired retina that is torn into the macula? I nodded. He said, One hundred percent.

I said, Well, I guess that's that.

After he drove us home I told Katya. The surgery would take around two hours. I found my will and my living will, telling doctors not to take heroic measures to save me. I called the office and talked to Jerome to let him know what was going on. I asked him whether he could call the judge's clerk to see about the possibility of putting off the hearing for a week or two. The next morning, Katya and I dropped Lincoln at a friend's house and she drove me to the hospital. At nine the anesthesiologist said I would begin to feel woozy in a minute or two. The last thoughts I had were: If I die, I wonder if Quaker will get a stay. Then: If I die, I'll have stumbled onto a guilt-free way of not doing this anymore.

Three hours later I woke up in the recovery room feeling like I'd eaten a bale of cotton. Katya and Lincoln were there, reading Narnia. Lincoln said, Look, Mama. Dada's awake. I smiled and tried to drink some water. It spilled out of my mouth. My tongue felt like wax paper. Lincoln said, Look what I brought. He held up a wishbone. Nana gave it to me. Let's break it, okay? He got the bigger piece, again.

I said, Amigo, are you cheating when we break these things?

He said, No, Dada, I am not. Do you want to know my wish? I nodded. He said, My wish is that you get to help the person you are trying to help.

■　■　■

THIS IS A LITTLE KNOWN FACT, but I invented books on tape. When I was in college, I said to myself, I should open a business renting out books on cassette tapes. It was my best idea, surpassing even my idea for a single serving of ground coffee that could be brewed in a bag like tea, for that fresh-brewed taste on camping trips. I also invented the idea of a computer in a car, with local maps programmed in, that could give you directions. I was going to put them in rental cars. Unfortunately, I took no steps in any of these instances other than having the idea, which apparently many other people had as well.

My grandmother was an avid reader. She went blind before there was such a thing as books on tape. She lost her vision when she was eighty-four and died when she was eighty-eight. She had cancer in her sinus that required radiation. The doctor told her she might lose her vision in the eye next to the sinus with the tumor. The doctor didn't say anything about losing the vision in the other eye. I wanted to sue. If I had been eighty-four and the doctor told me I would be blind, I'd take my chances with the cancer.

Death-penalty lawyers have a peculiar definition of victory. I already said that when my clients die of AIDS on death row, I count those deaths as victories. But it doesn't stop there. One of my clients was supposed to be executed on July 1. We got a stay on June 30, so he did not get executed until August 1. Another month of life in a sixty-square-foot cage. But he was breathing. That's a victory. When you lose most of the wars, you start seeing successes in individual battles as victories. In the free world, as my clients call it, definitions are different.

When I asked Charlie about the risks of the surgery, he told me I could lose my vision anyway. I said, I can't work if I can't see. He said that I'd learn to read Braille. I have a seven-year-old son and a wife I love. That seemed like a victory in my world.

Everybody sent me books on tape. I listened to the first book, written and read by David Sedaris. For five minutes I laughed out loud. Then I could not stop thinking about never being able to read again. Instead of hearing what he was saying, I was hearing him reading, and being reminded with every word that I could not read to myself. I did not listen to any more of the tapes.

■   ■   ■

For a week I worked with my eyes closed. Though I wouldn't want to stay that way, I have to say that my piano playing got much better, and my thinking was less clouded. Katya drove me to the office in the morning after dropping Lincoln at school, and I would lie on my couch and talk to Jerome, Gary, and Kassie about the case. Kassie felt sure Green was involved. She said, Woman's instincts. Trust me here.

It wasn't that I didn't trust her. Green was who I didn't trust. When I was in elementary school, my brothers and I would dial a random number and tell whoever answered not to pick up their phone for the next hour because the electric company was working on the line, and if they answered the phone, whoever was calling would get a severe shock. We'd wait ten minutes and dial the number again. Someone usually answered, and when they did, we'd scream like we'd been electrocuted. People torture others because it's fun, or because they don't have anything else to do, or because they're on death row, and they're angry and cold, and they aim to inflict as much pain as they can on the outside world before they get removed from it.

Two years earlier, a chaplain on death row started reading scripture to my clients. They began asking me to waive their appeals. The chaplain told them if they repented, Jesus would forgive them, but if they fought, they would burn in hell. In his universe, pursuing legal appeals was a form of fighting. By appealing, they were refusing to take responsibility for what they had done. Two times is a coincidence, three makes a conspiracy. After my fourth client wrote instructing me to waive his appeals, I drove to the chaplain's small house in Huntsville and sat in a rocking chair on the front porch, waiting for him to get home. I'm not a Christian, and if I were, I wouldn't be a good one. My capacity for turning the other cheek is shallow. I introduced myself and told him that if he spent another nanosecond with any of my clients, he'd learn for himself the ins and outs of litigation. He looked at me with what I first thought was incomprehension but later decided might have been sorrow, like I didn't know salvation when it was sharing my clothes.

Then again, even though I didn't want my clients surrendering their appeals, I had to admire the guy. He had gotten through to these men in a way no one had before. Sure, he had probably threatened them with eternal damnation, but still. I do believe he really did care about them. Almost all my clients should have been taken out of their homes when they were children. They weren't. Nobody had any interest in them until, as a result of nobody's having any interest in them, they became menaces, at which point society did become interested, if only to kill them. The chaplain had found a pressure point that could have saved lives, if someone had cared enough to find it sooner.

But there are a resolute handful who spurn saving. They make shanks from their dinner trays and they spit on the guards. They save their feces to use as projectiles. They make a game of breaking rules. Their objective is to die without breaking themselves. When Breaker Morant was marched before the firing squad, he told the bishop who had come to pray for him that he was a pagan, and he screamed at his executioners, Shoot straight, ya bloody bastards. Green was less literate, but just as incorrigible. The chaplain I threatened would never had gotten through to him.

Kassie had shown a picture of Green to Sandra Blue, the Quakers' neighbor. Blue told Kassie she had never seen him before, but Kassie wasn't sure. She decided to bluff. She paid Green a visit and told him that the Quakers' neighbor had recognized him. He squinted at her and shook his head. He told Kassie that if I didn't come up to see him, he was taking his secrets to the grave. Before she left he said, Sit there a few more minutes for me will you, and he dropped his hand into his lap.

She said, I swear, it's the last time I go talk to him. But you need to go see him. The scumbag knows something. I'm sure of it.

Jerome had gone back to Bud Lomax's house with a video camera. He sat in his car drinking coffee from six in the morning until he heard the TV through an open window at a quarter past ten. He knocked, and Lomax came to the door in his underwear. I watched the video. Lomax was unshaved but coherent. He was also believable. He looked at the camera and said, I don't believe that Henry Quaker killed my sister. I lied on him at his trial. I did it because that detective threatened me. He told me I had enough drugs in my house to spend the rest of my life in prison. I didn't want to spend no time in prison. I'm sorry. I'm so so sorry.

Gary had filed a motion requesting that we be allowed to retest some of the evidence in the case. When the court said we could, the prosecutor and I agreed that Melissa Harmon would take the samples to the lab. She called. She said, Two of the blood drops are too degraded to be useful. I'm waiting on results for the other four. Kimberly Crist thinks there is no doubt whatsover that the blood was dripping from a person or from an object that was moving from the woman toward the children.

Crist was the chief scientist at the lab. I did not welcome her opinion, especially the *no doubt whatsoever* language. But scientists are often wrong, even if they are never uncertain. I was not ready to give up on my theory, which of course was actually just a hope, until the remaining blood drops had been typed.

I said, If the blood belongs to one or both of the kids, she did it. If it belongs to her, the likely scenario is that she was shot first, and the killer went into the other room and then shot the kids. I'm not giving up on murder-suicide until we know whose DNA is in the blood.

Melissa said, The problem with your theory is that she couldn't have shot herself without a gun, but there was no gun.

I said, Maybe there was. There had to be. Why else test her hands?

I'm not sure.

I said, Would you be willing to talk to Wyatt?

Wyatt was the investigating detective. She said, Sure. Why not? It's your money.

I told the others about the call. Then I asked Gary to set up a trip to the prison for me to see Green and Quaker. I sat up and said, I'm walking next door to Treebeard's. Anyone want anything to eat? Gary said he'd go for me. I said, No, I want to go. I need to walk. I'll be back in ten minutes with shrimp étouffée and butter cake for everyone.

I stood at the counter while the servers filled quart containers with étouffée, gumbo, and rice. I felt a hand on my shoulder and turned around. It was Judge Truesdale. She looked at my eye.

Good God, what on earth happened to you? She touched my right cheek.

You should see the other guy, I said.

The server handed me my food. She said, I'm eating over there by myself. Sit with me for a minute. I followed her to her table. She said, This is off the record, okay?

I am pretty sure that off-the-record conversations with a judge who is presiding in a case that I have pending in her courtroom is not okay.

I said, Sure.

She said, Signing a death warrant makes things real to me. When the jury comes back and I announce a death sentence, I feel like a spectator. But when I sign the warrant... Her voice trailed off. She said, Quaker's jury was out for a long time. We thought they were going to acquit him.

I said, Why are you telling me this, Judge?

She said, I'm not exactly sure.

Then she said, In a hundred years, people are going to look back, and they are going to wonder what on earth we were doing. She drank some tea.

I said, I'll see you in a couple of weeks.

She said, Take care of that eye.

■   ■   ■

RICHARD FEYNMAN KEPT a list of the things he didn't know. I've often wondered how much you have to know to know what you don't know. I could make a list of things I want to know but don't, but it would depress me. I myself don't understand just about everything, a detail of which I'm reminded whenever I go to death row, especially when I go on Fridays. I was there to see Green, and to say hello to Quaker.

I pulled into the Exxon a couple of miles down the road from the prison. Inside, changing $10 bills for fists full of quarters, were three twenty-something-year-old women from France. A tall redhead, Monique, recognized me, said hello, and introduced me to her friends. They were in Texas to visit murderers. Monique was there to visit her husband, a Honduran who, along with three other drug dealers, had raped and murdered two high-school students who made a disastrously wrong turn down a dead-end street on the day that the older girl got her driver's license. The Honduran testified at his trial and said the murder was a mistake. He probably meant to say unplanned, in that it is hard to characterize as a mistake a murder that is accomplished by stabbing the victims thirteen times. I was less unforgiving before I became a dad. Monique met the guy after he arrived on death row. A year, four visits, and sixteen letters later, they got married by proxy. She had never touched him, and wouldn't, until he was dead.

I know two dozen murderers whose European wives fly over to see them three or four times a year, staying at cheap hotels near the prison and surviving on fast food and vending machines. The prison doesn't allow visitors to bring in reading material, so the women sit and twiddle their thumbs for an hour waiting for guards to bring out their spouses, then hold a grimy phone to their ears and talk to their mates through the Plexiglas for four hours more. They do not want to be U.S. citizens, so it might not be love, but it isn't expediency, either.

Monique asked me who I was going to see. I told her, and she told me that Green's wife was with him at that very moment. I had not known that Green had a wife. Monique told me her name was Destiny. She was Irish. I thought to myself, Who names their kid Destiny? Then I thought, How drunk would a woman have to be to get married to a guy who beat his previous wife to death?

Monique and her friends followed me to the prison. Outside the prison gates on Fridays, the parking lot is like a carnival. Vans and RVs and pickup trucks with campers fill all the visitor spaces. Because death row has visiting hours on Saturdays, families can see their loved ones two days in a row without missing two days of work. Wives come to see their husbands. Mothers and fathers come to see their sons. Sons and daughters come to see their dads. Death row on Fridays is living proof of how many families murderers ruin.

Before buzzing me through the gate, the guard reminded me that I could not wear sunglasses inside. I took them off so she could see my eye, the white of which was still the color of a fine chianti, three weeks after my surgery. She said, I think I'll let you wear them today, counselor.

Inside, Monique introduced me to Destiny. She couldn't have been much more than five feet tall, but she weighed, I would estimate, close to 300 pounds. Green weighed maybe 120. He was eating fried pork rinds and drinking a Pepsi. Destiny looked up at me when I walked over but didn't say a word. I said, Nice to meet you. She bit off a fingernail. Her skin was the color of liquid paper. She had put on lipstick, red as a candied apple. Half her ass fit on the folding metal chair. I picked up the other phone and told Green I'd talk to him in an attorney booth when he and his wife were finished visiting.

She said, I'm planning on being here all day, sweets. I told her that the prison would only let her visit for two more hours.

Green said, Introduce yourself to my new lawyer, Destiny. Then he winked at me.

I went and sat in the attorney booth and waited for the guards to bring Green in.

Death row has two types of attorney booths. One is a full-contact room. In this room, lawyers sit across a table from their clients. If you want to, you can shake your client's manacled hand or pat him on the shoulder. The room is usually used for psychological or psychiatric examinations. Next to it is the other kind of booth, a six-foot-by-four-foot box, that's divided down the middle by a concrete wall with a reinforced Plexiglas window. There's a padlocked mail slot that can be used to pass papers back and forth. You have to use a phone to converse. When they enter their half of the cage, inmates meticulously wipe off the mouth and ear pieces of the receiver with their white cloth jumpsuits. Death-row inmates are often obsessed with germs.

The main difference between an attorney area and a regular visiting cubicle is that, like those old-fashioned corner telephone booths, the attorney space is fully enclosed. The idea is to intimate the idea of privacy, and to prevent guards and others in the visiting area from hearing the conversation. Prison officials surreptitiously record visits between inmates and their nonlawyer visitors. They are not supposed to record attorney visits, but I wouldn't bet that they don't.

Green and I were conversing in a noncontact booth.

While he was squatting on his haunches, waiting for the guard to reach through a slot in the door and remove his handcuffs, Green said, What happened to you? I had forgotten how bad my eye looked. I told him nothing. Over the years I've had three or four clients I was actually fond of. Johnny Martinez was one of them. Green said, Did you know that Johnny Martinez and me were tight?

Death-row inmates live alone, sleep alone, shower alone. Once when I was in graduate school, I performed an experiment to see how long I could go without speaking another word to another human being. I made it eight days. I couldn't go to restaurants, and the grocery store was tough. At fast-food restaurants I would hold up fingers to place my order and nod when the worker handed me my food and thanked me. It's harder than you might think for a hardwired social animal to live without any human interaction. But death row hasn't always been that way. Until the late 1990s, death-row inmates could work outside their cells, in the prison laundry, for example, or fabricating license plates. They also had group exercise, so inmates could play basketball or handball, or lift weights together. Martinez was gay. For the gay inmates, or the temporarily gay, the old death row afforded social opportunities, so to speak. The implementation of total isolation was hard on Martinez. He told me, after the new regulations were put in place, that he never dreamed of escaping; he dreamed of being touched by a human being who wasn't a guard. I said, Yeah, Johnny, but the guys who aren't guards are murderers.

He said, Not all of them.

I said, I know. I was kidding.

He said, What do you dream about? I often didn't know what to say when Martinez asked me questions. I was useless to him as a lawyer. His case had been screwed up beyond repair by his previous attorneys. I told him that the first time we met. He didn't care. He wanted me to be his father, and his friend. I didn't want to be his friend just so I could feel better about the fact that, as his lawyer, I wasn't going to be able to save him. So I didn't say anything.

Johnny said, You do dream, right? He looked at me like I knew the answers to the big questions. I wrote a note on my pad so I had an excuse to look down. He twisted his head, trying to read it. He smiled. He said, I guess you can't dream if you don't sleep. Do you ever sleep?

When Quaker asked me that same question years later, he sounded curious. When Johnny asked, the question felt intimate. I didn't answer. He said, I bet you don't.

He said, I'd like to sleep, but it's loud up on level two.

Death row has three levels. Level 1 is where the well-behaved inmates live. Level 3 is for the troublemakers. Level 2 is in between. If Johnny was on level 2, he'd been doing something disruptive. That made no sense to me. He was meek and obedient. I said, What did you do to get moved?

He rubbed his face twice. His right thumb stroking one cheek two times, his other four fingers caressing the other. He had a wisp of scattered facial hair, like a teenager just starting to shave. He said, I wouldn't shave when the captain told me to. I asked him why not. He said, I'm not allowed to shave during Ramadan.

Johnny was raised a Catholic. He'd been an altar boy. His parish priest told me that he wanted to do whatever he could to help Johnny get off death row. He had already written the Pope, requesting papal intervention. I said, You're Catholic, aren't you?

He said, Not anymore. I'm Muslim now.

I said, Since when?

He smiled. It's who I am, Señor Abogado, he said to me.

I felt a piece of the wall crumble, and I said, I think you're the first Muslim I've met named Martinez. What does your family think? He tilted back his head and laughed. He seemed almost happy.

That was the image of him I tried to hold on to.

Green said, You remember Martinez, right? He told me you're a heretic.

Martinez did use to call me a heretic. He teased me. I had conversations with him that weren't about his case or the law. We talked about religion. I said it was bad, along with nationalism, the most regressive force in human society. He shook his head, respectful but adamant. He told me I might find myself praying every day if I was where he was. I told him he might be right, but that would just prove that I'm a hypocrite, not that I'm wrong. It was a running theme for us. If Green knew that Martinez called me a heretic, Martinez must have told him. But I didn't see Martinez and Green as friends.

I sat and waited. He said, Destiny doesn't trust you. I thought to myself, Destiny doesn't trust *me*? You've got to be kidding. She is a curious collection of DNA. She romanticizes murderers. She was attracted to you when the only thing she knew about you is that you're a murderer who beat your wife to death in front of your son. You might be something besides that—although I am not yet convinced—but Destiny didn't know that when she got your name and photograph and mailing address off an abolitionist Web site and decided to write you some sappy lovesick letter. So if Destiny doesn't trust me, partner, tell her the feeling's mutual.

My interior rant apparently amused me. I smirked. Green said, What's funny? I shook my head.

He said, So let's get to it. My wife is waiting. I took a pad out of my briefcase and licked the eraser on my pencil. But I didn't write anything down. There was no way I could forget what Green told me.

■　■　■

Hᴇ sᴀɪᴅ, Hᴇɴʀʏ Qᴜᴀᴋᴇʀ didn't kill no one. I asked him how
he knew that. He said, I told that girl who works for you that
Ruben did it. I just didn't exactly tell her how I know it. I know
he killed that family, 'cause I paid him to.

Green was not the first person to tell me he had gotten away
with murder. I've had several clients over the years who, as their
executions became imminent, made all sorts of exaggerated
claims. Billy Vickers went to his death taking credit for at least
a dozen murders. Henry Lee Lucas claimed hundreds. The
inaptly named Angel Resendiz, known to law-enforcement officials as the railway killer, rode the train from Kentucky to Texas
to California and back again, killing as many as fifteen people,
he said. Were these inmates clearing their consciences or trying to be memorable? My vote was for option two. I said nothing. Green said, What? You don't believe me? Go talk to Cantu.
Tell him you know about the gun he left there.

He bit off a fingernail and said to me, Bring any change
today, counselor?

Shit, I forgot again.

He spit the nail into his palm and looked at it. I said, You
shouldn't have told Destiny that I'm your lawyer. I can't be your
lawyer. There's a conflict of interest.

He nodded, put the nail back on his tongue and moved it
around in his mouth. He looked over my shoulder and nodded
his head toward my left. I turned around, but there was nobody
there. When I looked back at him, he was grinning.

He said, They taping this conversation? I told him they weren't
supposed to listen in on lawyers, but that they might be doing it

anyway. He said, Uh-huh. I waited for him to go on. I wanted to look at my watch, but fought it off, like not scratching an itch.

I thought to myself, He could be playing with me. If he is, I want to say nothing and seem uninterested. Then I thought, Or he could be telling the truth. If he is, I need to say nothing and figure out what to ask him. So I sat there, head swimming, saying nothing.

He said, Cantu is a dumb fuck. He killed the wrong person.

His story was not incredible. I'm not saying I believed him. I'm just saying he had hooked me. According to Green, Cantu sold drugs for him and occasionally threatened people who owed Green money. Green said that Cantu had claimed to have killed two dealers who stole from him, but Green did not know their names or whether it was true. He said that a woman named Tricia Cummings had been selling Ecstasy for him in a mixed neighborhood of blacks and Chicanos. She had been stealing from him. He didn't say how he knew that, and I didn't ask. He paused, like the rest would be obvious to me. I said, And?

He said, So I paid Cantu to kill her.

Cantu killed the wrong person. Green realized it as soon as Cantu told him that he also had to kill two kids because they saw him after he had killed the woman. Green didn't think Cummings had any kids and he knew she lived alone. He said he'd been to her house and slept with her, though he didn't say it quite like that.

If Green was telling the truth, Dorris Quaker died because she lived exactly two blocks east of someone who had been stealing from Green, and her kids had died because they were there, too.

His story made just enough sense for me to believe it. He said, You don't have to believe me. Ain't you the big DNA expert? I bet Cantu's DNA was all over the place.

I tried to think what evidence police had recovered that might have Cantu's DNA on it. The police report said that Dorris had been lying down or asleep when she was shot. There was no evidence she had struggled with anyone. So Cantu's skin wouldn't be under her fingernails. And unless Cantu had been injured, he wouldn't have left any blood. I doubted he pulled a beer out of the fridge when he was done, so I didn't expect to find his saliva on a beer bottle. Green said, Plus, Cantu's a talker. He probably told his old lady that he did it. I asked Green the name of Cantu's girlfriend. He said, I don't know, man. I don't even know if he has a girl. I'm just saying that if he does, he probably told her.

This conversation was becoming worthless to me. Then Green said, He left a gun there, like he was gonna trick the cops into thinking the bitch killed herself. Dumb fuck didn't leave the gun he used 'cause he said it was a good-luck charm. Left a piece he said was cold. What a dumb fuckin' Mexican.

I could feel myself losing the battle to beat back my need to believe him. I modified my goal. Instead of aspiring to nonchalance, I'd settle for exterior serenity. I said, And why are you telling me this now?

His face flexed and his lips made an *O*, like a fish in a tank breathing at the surface. I thought to myself, Be still. I was aiming for blankness. I didn't want Green to know what I was thinking before I knew myself. He said, What? You don't believe me?

I said, Thanks for the help, Green. I'll look into it.

He said, It's 'cause I like Quaker. He's next door to my house. I hear him reading words in there I don't understand, like it ain't even English. He might be going loco. His eye twitched into what I'm pretty sure was an involuntary wink. He said, You need me to sign something? I'll sign it.

I told him I'd talk to his lawyer and get back to him. He said, Come on, man. You know I ain't got that kind of time. I want you as my lawyer. My court-appointed lawyer's a piece of shit. His face changed and he suddenly looked angry. He said, Fuck this, man. He looked over my shoulder. I turned around. Destiny had gone. He said, Tell the guard I'm ready to go back to my house. I told him that I would. He said, And don't forget money next time.

■   ■   ■

WHEN I WAS in third grade, I stayed in the classroom to finish the book I was reading while everyone else lined up to go to the bathroom. Twenty minutes later, I had to go. I asked Mrs. Pittman for permission, and she told me I should have gone when the rest of the class did. I told her it was an emergency. She said that maybe next time I would not insist on playing by my own rules. I sat down at my desk and relieved myself through my pants. Half an hour later, the principal came in to check on our class. She walked around the room, looking over our shoulders at whatever we were working on. She got to my desk, paused, and then went and whispered something to Mrs. Pittman. Mrs.

Pittman grabbed me roughly by my elbow, and practically carried me to an empty desk next to Tommy Petite. He asked why I was there, and I told him there was something the matter with my chair. I looked back at my desk. There was a puddle of yellow under my seat.

That night after dinner I told my dad what had happened. He said, Sometimes it can be easy to confuse relief with revenge. Do you understand what I mean?

No, I don't think so.

He said, You need to make sure before you do anything that you can live with the consequences.

I said, I get it.

Green stood up to wait for the guards. I saw a stain of wetness around his crotch. I shook my head. I was looking forward to telling Kassie.

■　■　■

I GOT UP TO STRETCH my legs and clear my head while the guards took Green out and brought Quaker in. The door to the unisex bathroom swung open and Destiny walked out. She waved to Green as the guards were taking him away, then walked over to me, suddenly friendly. She said, Do you think Zeke will get his stay?

I thought to myself, Zeke? She calls him Zeke?

She was waiting for an answer. I hadn't known that Green already had an execution date, or whether his lawyer was fighting it. Had Green kept from me the fact that he had a date on purpose, or did he just assume that I already knew? It had to be the latter. My office keeps track of all executions. His name was probably on a document lost on my desk. He would assume that I knew before he had that his execution had been scheduled. But that didn't answer my primary question: Was his claim of responsibility just a ploy to get a stay? He had to have figured that I would want a stay for him so I could help Quaker with whatever he knew, and he was right about that. He was proving to be a skilled manipulator, and I was feeling good about myself for disliking him from the get-go. I needed to know when the date was, but I didn't want to ask her.

I said, I hope so. I'm guessing that he will. She stuck out her hand and I shook it. She held on a little too long then spun around like a fashion model and wordlessly walked away.

◼ ◼ ◼

QUAKER WAS JOKING with the guards when they brought him into the visiting booth. I read a story about a cop who investigated serial killings. He would spend hours and hours interviewing notorious serial killers, getting close to them, revealing secrets in order to be trusted, and they would reward him by reporting the details of their crimes—grisly, horrific details, details that would keep me awake for a week, maybe forever. But the cop couldn't be a cop if he was like that. The cop told the author that he put these conversations in a compartment of his brain and locked them away immediately, so that by the time he got out to his car, he was thinking about which Mexican restaurant he'd go to for lunch. Were Quaker's jailers like that? Would they be able to wall off their relationship with him and numbly escort him to the gurney? I knew their numbers and addresses, and I was going to have to find out. It might not help, but it definitely wouldn't hurt, for the guards to say that they thought Quaker was innocent, for them at least to say that he shouldn't die.

. He rubbed his wrists where they had been cuffed. He leaned toward me and looked at my eye. Man, he said, you look like ET.

I said, You know a guy on the row named Ezekiel Green?

He said, I know of him.

I said, What do you know?

Why's it matter?

I'm just curious.

He said, The guys in here who ain't too bright think he's like a prophet or something.

Yeah.

The other guys think he's insane.

I said, Which group are you in?

He smiled. Hey, I'm no genius like you, but I'm on your side of the bell curve.

I said, So you think he's insane.

He said, It's just based on what I heard. Like I said, I ain't never had much of a conversation with the guy. He's next to me on the pod, and I hear him talking on the phone and shit, and he doesn't seem crazy. The words make sense, you know what I mean? I nodded. Quaker said, Why you wanna know?

I said, He just told me who murdered Dorris and your kids. He said it was a case of mistaken identity.

■   ■   ■

On the way back to my office I called Katya. She asked, What did he say?

I told her that his mouth literally fell open. His chest sagged, his chin jutted forward, and his lower jaw just fell. I thought it was just a figure of speech. But it was an actual physical reaction. His jaw really dropped. He started to say something, I think his lips actually moved, but no sound came out. Then he rubbed his eyes, using the knuckles on his index fingers. Finally he said, Why?

I didn't know whether he was asking me why Green had told me, or whether it was a more Job-like question. I told him everything Green had said, including about hearing Quaker talking to himself in a foreign language. My voice was flat, like maybe I believed him, maybe I didn't. Quaker said, It ain't no foreign language. I got a book of Wallace Stevens poems and I read them out loud. I don't know what half the words mean but I like the way they sound.

He started crying. The only reason I could tell at first was that his chest was heaving, like he was out of breath from sprinting. Then I saw the tears. He kept saying, My poor babies, my poor babies, my love. Over and over. I didn't know what to say. I just sat there.

He said, After the explosion, my company sent me to some-place near New Braunfels. The shrink said I had PTSD. But you already know that, right? It was like *One Flew Over the Cuckoo's Nest*. You seen that movie? All these old people walking around. They were mostly German, I think. I couldn't understand nothing they were saying. Anyway, one night I was sitting on the balcony smok-ing some weed and thinking about how I could just disappear in that town, it's beautiful there, maybe walk off into the moun-tains, and nobody would ever miss me. You ever feel like that? That you could die and no one would even know? They'd proba-bly look for me for a while, but they'd stop eventually. Then it was like Dorris and Danny and Charisse was standing there. I could feel 'em there, actually *feel* 'em. *They'd* miss me. It saved me to be thinking that. I swear to God it did. I wanted to watch Danny and Charisse graduate, be a grandpa, get old with Dorris.

Katya said, He didn't do it, you know. I don't know whether Green was telling you the truth, but your client didn't kill his family.

I said, I know. I am sorry to say that I know that.

■ ■ ■

TWO MORNINGS LATER Lincoln came into our room at five. I was still sleeping. He said, Dada, can I get up now?

I said, Linco, it's Sunday. I want to sleep a little longer. He said he wasn't tired. I told him he could stay up if he'd go with me for a run when it got light.

He said, But Dada, I'm too big for the stroller thing, and it's too far for me to ride my bike.

He had me there, so I got up, got dressed, and went out while it was still night, just the dog and me, and told Linco not to bother his mama unless it was an emergency.

From the time Lincoln could hold his head up until he was five, I would take him with me in the stroller when I would go jogging on weekends. I hate jogging. When I'm swimming or rowing, my mind wanders, and solutions to problems come to me, at least sometimes. When I'm jogging, all I'm thinking about is finishing. Jogging with Lincoln changed all that. I would tell him stories before he could talk, and listen to his stories later. He and Winona and I would run around a mile-and-a-half loop. We'd usually run three laps, and I wouldn't even notice how much my knees were hurting. Some days, when I felt fresh and it wasn't too hot, I'd say to Lincoln, as we were finishing up lap number three, Hey, amigo, how about another circle today?

One morning he asked, Dada, why do you like running so much?

I said, Actually, Linco, I hate running. But I like hanging out with you.

He said, But you can hang out with me at the house.

I said, Yeah, that's true, but I want to hang out with you for a lot more years, and if I jog, I think I'll have more years with you.

He said, Okay, then. Let's run one more loop. But faster this time, okay? I'd sprint for as long as I could manage, and he'd say, Wheeeee.

He and Katya would be leaving for the beach later that day. I had the Quaker hearing coming up, a looming execution date for O'Neill, and the possibility that Green would get executed before I could learn whether he was lying or telling the truth, or whether he knew any more truth, or, for that matter, any truth at all, that could help me. I felt myself sinking. There was nothing I could do about anything. Three people were going to die in a month because I was completely out of ideas. I thought to myself, I should have gone rowing.

■　■　■

KATYA HAS A CHILDHOOD FRIEND who grew up to be an artist you've probably heard of. They're like college roommates. They talk and text and e-mail every day. Sometimes I'm jealous of their closeness. I don't have any friends like that, except Katya and Lincoln, and the dog. Ten years ago, we were in New York at my law-school reunion, and the artist invited us to dinner at her fancy apartment. Katya had told her that I like to cook. Almost as soon as we were introduced, the artist asked me to make a pitcher of martinis, and after I mixed them and poured three glasses, she told me how to light the grill, where the salad ingredients were, and that she liked her steak so rare that it would still moo. (I did not hold this against her; Katya likes hers the same way.) The two of them went one way, carrying their glasses and the pitcher, and I stayed in the kitchen, looking for the tools I needed to make dinner. By the time I brought the food to the living room, where we ate off a coffee table while sitting on the floor and watching *America's Next Top Model*, Katya and the artist were drunk as skunks.

I mention the point about inebriation solely for the sake of lending credibility to what I am about to say: This artist is a detestable human being. My experience is that drunk people don't lie, and in her drunken state, she was racist, anti-Semitic, homophobic, narcissistic, and altogether unlikable. Twenty years before, while she was involved in a relationship with two other people (who might or might not have known about one another), she got pregnant by a third—well, at least she thinks it was the third. You might consider it a sign of redemption that she agreed to marry the probable father, except that she started cheating again a month after their kid was born.

I'm a libertarian. If people want to be married to lecherous spouses, let them. But my own life is too short to waste even the briefest moment with people like her, and that would be true no matter how long my life happens to be.

When we were back in Houston, and enough time had passed, I told Katya I was amazed that she could be friends with this terrible person. She said, She's been my friend since she was eight years old, which is way before she was a terrible person. What am I supposed to do? Abandon her? There are beautiful things about her I know about that you don't, because you are too judgmental to see them. If you have a friend, you have to take them as they are.

There's not really anything I could say to that. I am judgmental. I've already admitted as much. We agreed to disagree about the artist. The next time we were in New York, I stayed at the hotel bar while Katya and she went to dinner.

I have a theory about great artists, which is that they are ordinarily awful human beings. To be a great artist, you have to be so self-centered, so indifferent to everything but your own artistic sensibility, that the whole world, including the people who love you, are just means to your end. Too bad it doesn't work in reverse. Wouldn't it be terrific if you could become a great writer or painter or musician by being a shitty person? And don't write me with a list of exceptions; I am aware that there are some. All I am saying is that in general, my advice to you is that if you should meet a famous artist, do not go to her house for dinner.

But clichés are clichés for a reason, and that dark cloud too had its silver lining. Dinner at the famous artist's house changed me as a death-penalty lawyer. Until I met her, my focus was on the law, on why some legal rule or principle meant that my client should get a new trial. I'd do exhaustive research, write a powerful legal argument, and then watch no one pay it any heed. The problem with this lawyerly approach is that nobody cares about rules or principles when they're dealing with a murderer. The lawyer says that the Constitution was violated every which way, and the judge says, Yeah, but your client killed somebody, right? For all our so-called progress, the tribal vengefulness that we think of as limited to backward African countries is still how our legal system works. Deuteronomy trumps the Sixth Amendment every time. Prosecutors and judges kowtow to family members of murder victims who demand an eye for an eye, and the lonely lawyer declaiming about proper procedures is a shouting lunatic in the asylum whom people look at curiously and then walk on by.

Then (if I might say so myself) I had a perfectly cooked piece of grass-fed sirloin while sitting on the floor of the racist artist's brownstone, and my entire focus changed. My clients were better people than this piece of garbage, and they even killed somebody. That was the magic moment my focus changed. My clients did a terrible, sometimes unforgivable, thing, but most of them were worth saving. It was a moral realization, not a legal epiphany. Sometimes the most immoral, detestable person you've ever met can teach you an ethical lesson worth knowing. That's a lesson, too.

■　■　■

LINCOLN AND KATYA had gone to Galveston. They even took the dog, which was good for the three of them but bad for me, because it meant that when I talked to myself, the dog was not in the room, so I could not pretend that I wasn't.

It was January 5. On the wall calendar in my office, I had four dates circled in red. O'Neill was scheduled to be executed in one week, on January 12. Green was scheduled to get executed three days later, on January 15. Quaker was scheduled for execution on February 4, and we had his hearing in the trial court on January 27. A typical month had three or four dates with marks-a-lot circles. It was a fairly ordinary agenda for a death-penalty lawyer in Texas.

I took two chocolate glazed donuts out of the Shipley's box. Kassie said, Two donuts? That's a record.

I said, Katya and Lincoln took all our food to Galveston. All I've got at home are oranges, coffee, ice cream, beer, peanuts, and bourbon. And I'm pacing myself.

Kassie said that she would try to locate Tricia Cummings, the woman that Green said was supposed to have been killed by Cantu. Gary was going to try to find Cantu and take another run at him. I told him that he needed to take Melissa Harmon with him. I was going to call Melissa to tell her about the story that Cantu had left a gun at the scene, and to see whether she could have a chat with Detective Wyatt.

Jerome said, What about me?

I didn't want him doing anything that couldn't be inter-rupted, because I had a feeling that O'Neill was going to cause some interruptions. I said I thought he had his hands full with O'Neill. He said there was nothing left to do but wait. I said, Fine, help Kassie track down Cummings. He looked at me like I had just asked him to rinse out the coffee mugs, but he didn't say anything. I said, All right, fine. Can you also follow up on the blood? The lab never did call me back. He nodded and almost smiled, slightly mollified.

Melissa Harmon and I met for breakfast the next morning at the Buffalo Grille. I was eating oatmeal. She was eating chick-en-fried steak and fried eggs. I said, You're a real health freak.

She said, Steak and eggs is a classic. You want some?

I shook my head. I told her about my conversation with Green and asked her if she would be willing to talk to Wyatt about the gun. She slowly chewed a piece of meat. After she swallowed it she said, Can you think of a way for me to have that conversation without accusing him of something unethical?

I said, If I could think of that, I'd have the conversation with him myself instead of paying your exorbitant rates.

She smiled. She said, So what's it like always representing the bad guys?

I said, I'm pretty sure that one of my guys isn't actually bad.

■   ■   ■

GARY CALLED. He and Harmon had gone to the house where I talked to Cantu. Gary said that the house was empty. There was a mattress on the bedroom floor, half a roll of toilet paper on the bathroom floor, two slices of leftover sausage pizza in the refrigerator, and a half-gallon carton of Tropicana orange juice, two-thirds gone, on the counter. That's it. No clothes, nothing to read, no TV or radio, no towels, no beer. Cantu was gone.

While Gary looked through the house and took inventory, Melissa talked to the neighbors. No one knew his name. No one had any idea where he'd gone. I asked Gary to take the orange juice. Maybe Cantu drank from the carton. Maybe we could get some DNA. I didn't have any idea what good it would do us, but I figured it couldn't hurt.

As I was hanging up, Jerome, ever the meticulous one, came into my office waving a single piece of paper. I said, What's that? He said he had been going through the file of Quaker's trial lawyer. It was a page from Detective Wyatt's report. I wondered how I had missed it. Probably because I read through the file before I knew who Cantu was. Either way, it was not exactly a confidence booster. The report indicated that Wyatt had interviewed Cantu. It didn't say why. In the report Wyatt had noted that Cantu had an alibi. But it didn't say what the alibi was, or why Wyatt had even bothered interviewing Cantu in the first place.

Most important of all, though, the fact that the report was in the trial lawyer's file meant that the trial lawyer had it, and that meant we could not accuse the state of withholding relevant evidence. One of our legal claims had just disappeared.

I told Jerome what Gary had learned at Cantu's former house.

He said, That's too bad, but it really doesn't matter. It's not like he was all of a sudden going to admit to killing three people.

Jerome is also the guy in the office who can be counted on to remind me that the way our lives actually work is not how death-penalty cases get portrayed on TV. I said, I've got a story that ain't got no moral. He looked at me oddly. I said, You know, let the bad guy win every once in a while? His look didn't change. I said, It's Billy Preston, man.

Jerome has an iPod that has something like fifteen thousand songs on it. He plays guitar in a garage band. He said, Who's that?

I shook my head. He put the piece of paper on my desk and walked out.

■ ■ ■

GREEN'S LAWYER WAS Mark Roberts, one of the smartest, most aggressive death-penalty lawyers around. When Green first wrote asking to see me, I called Roberts to make sure it was okay with him. The fact that Green didn't like him was yet another fact that made me feel better about my first instinct. I called Roberts and told him about Green's claim of responsibility. I knew what he would say if I asked him to allow me to get a written statement from Green. He'd say no. The reason is that he had asked the parole board to commute Green's sentence to life in prison, and he had filed another writ with the Supreme Court. Logically and legally speaking, whether Green did or did not tell Cantu to kill Tricia Cummings had no bearing on either one of those last-ditch efforts. Realistically speaking, it mattered a lot. If there was some parole-board member who was inclined toward leniency, or if there was some Supreme Court justice who was intrigued by Mark's legal argument, the inclination and intrigue would give way to disgust and abhorrence if Green was connected to three more murders, especially when two of them were children. I asked him anyway. He said, Green is a piece of shit. I'm tempted. But sorry, Doc, no can do. I told him thanks anyway.

In Thursday's mail I got a handwritten statement from Green, largely repeating what he had told me in person. His execution was a week away. I called Mark again. Green was a goner. There was no chance whatsoever that he would be alive the following Friday, so I made what I believed to be a costless offer. I wanted to get Green to tell his story while hooked up to a polygraph. Polygraph evidence is inadmissible in court, but I wasn't thinking about that. I was thinking that if his confession held up, the parole board or the governor would feel safer granting Quaker relief. I said to Roberts, Here's what I'd like to do. I'll have Green polygraphed tomorrow, but I won't use the results until after he's executed.

Roberts said, You mean if he's executed.

I said, Yeah, that's what I mean. If he's executed.

Roberts said, If it's okay with Green, it's okay with me.

■   ■   ■

THAT AFTERNOON I rode the Metro train from my office to the medical center to have Charlie look at my eye. I was reading some papers we planned to file the next day in the O'Neill case. I did not have my new glasses yet. I was holding the pages so close to my face that they were touching my nose. A thick Hispanic woman was breast-feeding an infant. Sitting next to her was a boy who looked to be about eight. He was beautiful, part Latino and part black. I looked down at what I was reading and heard him say, Mire, Mama. His mother said, Shh. The boy said, Mama, ese hombre es ciego. I looked up. The boy was pointing at me. I gave him a smile, waved surreptitiously with two fingers, then covered my eyes with my hands and peeked over them at him. He could tell his friends that he played peek-a-boo with a blind man. He smiled back, and his mother looked at me warmly.

Charlie had told me that I would be able to go back to work

forty-eight hours after the surgery, but that I would get headaches for a while. He asked how I was doing. I told him I had a splitting headache. He said, Yes. I told you that would happen. It's perfectly normal. He had been using an instrument to look at the back of my eye, where he had reattached the retina. He pushed back from the machine he had been looking through. He said, Well, the front of the eye still looks like hamburger, but the back looks beautiful. Your retina is better now than when you were born. I told him the headaches made it hard to concentrate, and I asked him how long they would last. He said, Buy a month's worth of aspirin.

I said, A month? Are you serious?

He said, You've always been an impatient SOB.

I said, Yeah, but a grateful one. I shook his hand and left.

■   ■   ■

I TOOK THE TRAIN back to my office but decided not to go back upstairs. I got in my car intending to go home. Kassie had gotten special permission from the warden to polygraph Green the next morning. I needed to spend some time thinking about what questions to ask him.

I called Jerome to talk about O'Neill. O'Neill's execution was four days away. We had asked the state court to halt the execution on the grounds that O'Neill had descended so deeply into the darkness of madness that he was immune from execution. The court denied our motion, saying we had waited too long to

raise the issue of O'Neill's sanity. We immediately filed a petition in federal court, but it was just sitting there. Jerome asked
when I thought we'd hear something. I said, I'm guessing at
about five forty-five on Monday. That means we can call him
when we get denied and he'll get a whole quarter hour to get
ready to die. Jerome asked me if I would have time to visit with
him when I was at the prison the next day.

I said, If he's really convinced he isn't going to be executed,
what's the point of my telling him good-bye?

Jerome said, I promise you, the guy is crazy. I think he really
is Ford incompetent. But just humor me, okay?

Jerome was referring to a case called *Ford versus Wainwright*.
In that case, the U.S. Supreme Court said that a state cannot execute someone if the person does not know why he is in prison
nor that the state is planning on killing him. The decision is an
example of a lofty principle that has almost no practical appli-
cation. Someone can be the most disturbed person you have
ever known, yet not be Ford incompetent. Everyone has heard
the story about Ricky Rector. He was a death-row inmate in
Arkansas who always saved his dinner's dessert to eat for breakfast the next day. During the 1992 presidential campaign, when
Bill Clinton was still trying to secure the Democratic nomina-
tion, he flew back to Arkansas to preside over the Rector execution. After the lethal injection, the guards went to clean out
Rector's cell. They found the piece of pecan pie that Rector had
requested with his final meal. Rector had put it on the table
next to his cot, to save it for the breakfast he was apparently
expecting to have the morning following his execution.

Convincing a judge that someone is Ford incompetent is a

daunting proposition. I said, Don't worry, Jerome. I'm kidding. I'll let him know what to expect.

I knew a girl who used to live two blocks from me. I would see her getting the paper in the morning when I was out with the dog. She would always seem a little embarrassed to be seen in her bathrobe, but she would always pet Winona. She and her husband had triplets. An instant family, she once said to me. One evening he took the kids to watch the Astros play in their new stadium. He was driving over the Pierce elevated highway when an 18-wheeler driven by a driver who had been on the road for nineteen straight hours nudged his SUV off the road. The car fell onto the street below and burst into flames. The man and the three children burned to death. She moved out of the house, and I had not seen her since. I glanced down to break the connection on my call with Jerome. I looked up just as a woman carrying two bags of groceries was stepping off the curb. My light was green. I leaned on the horn and called her a name I'd rather not repeat. When I looked at her in the rearview mirror, I could have sworn that she was my friend, and that the look on her face was not fear, but regret.

Instead of driving home to my empty house, I drove to McElroy's pub, bought a strong Honduran cigar, and ordered a double of Woodford Reserve, neat. I finished it and ordered another. The woman sitting two stools down from me had a plate of olives and cheese in front of her. She was drinking scotch out of a highball glass and chewing on a piece of ice. When the bartender looked at her, she pointed to her glass. I moved over next to her and said, Judge Truesdale?

She swiveled in her chair and looked at me. She was fifteen

years younger than the judge. She said, Afraid not. I think you confused me with someone. She looked at the wedding band on my left hand and swiveled back around.

I said, Sorry about that. I paid my check and left.

I picked up some tacos from a taco stand but felt sick to my stomach when I got home and left them on the counter. I stood in the hot shower until the hot water ran out then got in bed to watch the nine o'clock news. Instead I fell immediately asleep and had a dream. Katya and I were in Las Vegas. I was playing terrible poker, but I couldn't lose. From middle position I would raise with an unsuited eight-five, and three eights would come on the flop. Spectators were gathering around the table to watch, like I was a magician. I felt gleeful, and also embarrassed. I looked at my watch. Katya and I were meeting at seven to go to dinner, and it was almost eight. I cashed in my chips and rushed upstairs. Everything was okay. Katya was still in the shower. I lay down on the bed and poured myself a drink. I dozed off, and when I woke up, the shower was off and Katya was kissing my chest. I put my hands on either side of her head. Her lips felt unfamiliar. I opened my eyes and she was gone. A strange woman with her back to me was sitting naked on the edge of the bed. She turned around. Judge Truesdale said, What time will your wife be back?

The ringing phone woke me.

Lincoln said, Hi, Dada. When are you going to call to tell me good night? I looked at the clock. It was nine thirty.

I said, I thought you would already be asleep, amigo. Why are you still up?

He said, Mama and I went to a restaurant and ordered pizza and it took a really long time.

I said, Okay, amigo. I'm glad you called, but you have to go to sleep now, okay? Can I talk to Mama?

He said, Sure. Good night. I love you.

Katya got on the phone. She said, How's everything going?

I told her I didn't have a clue but that there was nothing I could do that weekend and that I was planning to drive down to the beach when I left the prison the next day and stay until Monday morning. She asked whether she should tell Lincoln or whether it was going to be a surprise. I said, Go ahead and tell him.

I think I was already planning to go to Galveston before the dream. But I can't be sure. Half the things I do in life are for reasons I can't fathom.

■   ■   ■

I STAYED UP the rest of the night thinking about how to approach Green. Claiming partial responsibility for three murders he was not suspected of would be a ridiculous long-term strategy, even if it got his life extended past Thursday. Normally, that would count in favor of his credibility. But death-row inmates live their lives in thirty-day increments. There isn't any long-term strategy, at least for the vast majority who are not actually innocent. The focus is on avoiding the looming execution date. Everything else can wait. You solve the immediate problem, and don't think about the next one. Or, as we say in my office, we'll burn the distant bridges when we get to them.

Maybe I could understand Green's motivation and assess his veracity if I could crawl inside his life, but I could not get inside his life even if I wanted to, and on top of that, I didn't want to. He killed his son's mother and grandmother with his bare hands. Who can relate to that? Who wants to? When I leave the prison, I can hardly wait to get in the shower and wash the death and deprivation off of me. I hire experts to tell judges what it is like to be one of my clients, and while they are talking, I try hard not to listen. My job is to keep them from being executed, not to save them, or to heal them. My job is hard enough, but at least it is possible. I'm not Don Quixote.

Understanding a broken human being in a visceral way means that you are broken, too, at least for a while. I do not want to imagine abusing my son, or imagine being abused by my father. I don't want to think about what kind of person would commit that abuse, or what kind of person could, or what would happen to the person who received it. But you don't get to control the thoughts that enter your mind, and I couldn't stop myself from picturing Green as a kid Lincoln's age. Green's sister was a sociology professor at the University of Miami. What did someone do to him to make him a monster?

The guard at the entrance to the visitor's lot asked me to open my hood and my trunk. There was a leash and water bowl for the dog, and the board game Candyland. This vehicle search was a new part of the routine. I got out of the car while the guard looked at the engine block. I asked him what was the purpose. He said, Looking for people who don't belong. I chuckled at that. I said that it seemed to me that it would make more sense to search cars when they were leaving the prison, rather than when they were arriving. He didn't laugh. No one gets my jokes.

■   ■   ■

KASSIE WAS ALREADY THERE, sitting next to Destiny, explaining to Green how everything would work once the polygraph examiner arrived. I said hello and walked over to talk to O'Neill. He was visiting with his parents. They had not seen him in six years. Thinking it was going to be their last chance to see him alive, they had driven down from Michigan and were living at a rest stop in their RV. I introduced myself. His mother hugged me. His father took my right hand in both of his and shook it. His mom said, Thank you for everything you are doing for Ronnie. I didn't tell her that my vote at the office had been to do nothing. Instead I told her we would do what we could. I sat down to talk to O'Neill. His parents stood behind me so they could listen, too. I told them just to ask if they had any questions. O'Neill's mom said, Thank you, sir.

O'Neill had three cans of Coke, two bags of nacho-cheese-flavored Doritos, two bags of Funions, and three Snickers bars arranged in front of him. He was making sandwiches by layering a tortilla chip, a piece of chocolate bar, a Funion, another piece of chocolate, and another Dorito. Then he'd pop the whole thing into his mouth. His head would rotate like a figure eight while he chewed. He ate a sandwich, wiped the front of his lower teeth using his tongue, then he said to me, Good day, sir. Those are my parents standing right behind you. I told him I knew, that we had met just moments before. He said, I am not sure you are understanding me, sir. Shall the potter be regarded as the clay? That the thing made should say of its maker, He did not make me? Or the thing formed say of Him who made it, He has not understanding?

I exhaled loudly and shook my head like I was clearing cobwebs. His father leaned close to me and whispered, It's Isaiah.

I said, a little too harshly, I know that. Chapter twenty-nine. What I'm trying to figure out is the connection.

He said, Oh. I'm sorry. Well, I don't think there is one.

O'Neill looked at his father like he'd never seen him before, his eyes blank, his pupils the size of a pinhead. I tried to make eye contact, but his gaze was off to my left, like he was examining my ear. He gave no indication that he remembered me. I felt like Bill Murray in *Groundhog Day*. I explained that we had filed something, that we were raising a Ford claim and challenging his competency to be executed, that we probably would not hear from the courts until Monday morning, that by the time we prepared our emergency appeal to the Supreme Court and heard back from them, it would be close to 6:00 p.m. I said it all in one breath. Behind me, I heard his mother gasp.

O'Neill's head twitched ever so slightly to the right, and he stared at my eyes. Then his gaze dropped to my chest and lingered. He said, I can see you have a good and pure heart, sir, and I thank you. But I shall not require your interventions or entreaties on my behalf. I am watched over and blessed. These men cannot do me harm. He waved his arms like a windmill.

He bent over and put his ear next to a sandwich he had built, the way you lean toward someone who's whispering. I told him I would talk to him the following week.

As I was leaving, I wrote down his dad's cell phone number and promised him I would call as soon as I heard something from the Supreme Court. His eyes were wet. His wife was holding on to her purse strap so tightly that her knuckles were white. She said, Ask him, dear.

He took a hold of my upper arm. I could smell peanut butter and jelly on his breath. He said, We are not planning to watch it. We'll be at the prison, but we want to stay outside in the camper. Do you think that's all right?

Against my better judgment I said, I am not convinced it is going to happen, Mr. O'Neill. If it does, though, you and your wife should not watch.

He nodded his head up and down twice. His wife stifled a sob. I squeezed his shoulder, and I walked away.

■   ■   ■

THREE GUARDS BROUGHT Green into a room I had never been in. Two walked on either side of him, holding his arms, and one walked two steps behind. Green's wrists were cuffed and chained to a leather belt around his waist. Because his ankles were also chained, he did not so much walk into the room as shuffle. When he walked through the door, he smiled, revealing a gold canine tooth I had not noticed before. In the center of the room was a small, square bridge table, with two folding chairs, across from one another. Against the wall were two plastic chairs, the kind you can buy for $10 at the grocery store. Kassie was with me, along with Fred Faison, the polygraph examiner. Green looked at Kassie and grinned. He nodded to me and said, This is the first time since I got here that I been in a room with people from the free world who ain't guards. Then he turned to the guard on his left and said, Y'all gonna unchain me? The guard did not say anything. He turned around and looked at the captain. The captain also said nothing and walked out of the room.

Kassie asked Faison in a whisper whether he needed Green to be uncuffed to do the testing. Faison shrugged and said, Not really. Either way will be fine.

The captain walked back in. He said, Warden wants Green to stay chained.

Green said, That's bullshit, man. I ain't doing this in chains.

I asked the captain whether I could talk to Green privately. He stepped back toward the door, and motioned the other two guards over to him. *Privately* apparently meant they'd give me eight or ten feet of space. I stood between Green and the guards, so that my back was to them. I said, I've got other shit I can be doing today. To be honest, I don't think you will pass the polygraph, and if you do, I don't think it will matter. So I don't really care what you decide, but will you hurry up and make a decision so I can get on with my day?

He said, You bring any change, counselor?

Kassie was standing next to me. She quickly said, I can buy you a soda.

Green kept his eyes on me and smiled. He said, A Dr. Pepper and a Sprite. He paused a beat, then said, Please.

Kassie walked out to get them. Green looked at the captain and said, I'm ready.

I sat on the edge of one of the plastic chairs, trying to decide whether I believed a word he was saying, trying to figure out whether I could use it, trying to divine his motives. Faison was staring down at his machines as he asked Green a series of questions in a robotic monotone. He had placed sensors on Green's chest and head. A blood pressure cuff encased his left biceps. After every question, before he gave an answer, Green leaned forward and sipped from one of his drinks, alternating between the two. After half an hour, Faison stood up and walked over to me. Anything else you want me to cover? he asked. I looked at Kassie. She shrugged. I told Faison I thought we had enough. He walked back over to Green and started to remove the wires.

Green said, We done? Faison said that we were. Two guards were immediately on either side of Green, holding on to his elbows as he rose from the chair. I stood up to leave. Green looked at Kassie and said, Thanks for the sodas. To me he said, I'm trying to help you here.

■   ■   ■

LINCOLN PICKED UP the extension while I was talking to Katya. He said, Hi, Dada. Did you have a good day at the death row?

I told him it was a sad day. He said, Oh. Well, guess what?

Mama and I took Winona for a walk on the beach. It was really long. And even though it's not very hot outside, Winona got so hot that she went swimming. And there was steam coming off her. And Dada, the water is freezing. I asked him whether he would be ready for another walk when I got to the beach. He said, That would be nice.

Just as I was arriving at the cabin, at nearly five o'clock, Jerome called. He said, The judge ruled against us in O'Neill, and the clerk from the federal court of appeals called. They said that if we plan to file an appeal, it has to be there by five tomorrow.

The next day was Saturday. I asked Jerome whether he was sure that was what the clerk said. He said, I can e-mail you the order if you want me to. I told him that I'd be at the office by noon.

Upstairs, Katya was in the kitchen making cookie dough. Lincoln was licking the beater, and Katya was giving cherry-size pieces to Winona. I said, Looks like you guys will have enough energy for a superlong walk.

Lincoln said, Yippee.

I cut off the end of a cigar. When Lincoln, Winona, and I got outside, I lit it. Winona went running off ahead, chasing sand-crab smells. Lincoln said, Dada, please don't smoke that.

I said, Amigo, I don't smoke very many anymore, and I like how they taste, and they help me to relax. Lincoln and I were holding hands.

Winona circled back around to us. She had found a tennis ball. Her snout was covered with muddy sand. Lincoln said, Dada, if you smoke cigars you're not going to be able to spend as much time with me.

I said, You're a smart kid, amigo. I held the cigar until it burned itself out.

Lincoln said, Thank you, Dada.

■　■　■

AFTER LINCOLN WENT to bed, Katya and I sat outside on the deck with a pitcher of margaritas while the steaks were on the grill. It was cold, but not uncomfortable. The sky was clear, and we could see Orion, Taurus, and, inside the bull, the cluster of blue stars known as the Pleiades. I told her about O'Neill and that I would have to drive back to Houston first thing in the morning. She said, Do you really think the judges will be working this weekend?

I said, Of course not. This is their way of saying fuck you to us.

We sat and looked at the sky. I said, I saw O'Neill this morning. He did not remember me at all. He was randomly quoting from the Bible. At least it seemed random. His dad knew it was from Isaiah. They don't want to watch the execution.

Katya lifted my right hand and put it in her lap. She said, In my astronomy class, I had to calculate the age of the Pleiades. The only time I could ever do math was when it involved the stars. I asked her how old they were. She said, I don't remember exactly. I think one hundred million years or so. If it weren't for Lincoln, that would change my perspective on the meaning of everything.

I said, It's funny O'Neill was quoting Isaiah. The Pleiades are mentioned in the Book of Amos. You who turn justice into wormwood, and hurl righteousness to the ground. Seems appropriate, doesn't it.

She said, I don't know about Amos, but the Red Hot Chili Peppers sang about them. Wanna hear?

I smiled. I'll take a pass, gorgeous.

She said, Why don't you take the steaks off the grill and let them rest in the kitchen for a while?

I said, That is the perfect idea.

Later, while we were still lying in bed, I told her about the polygraph examination. Green answered yes when Faison asked him whether he had personal knowledge about the deaths of the Quaker family. He answered yes when asked if Ruben Cantu killed them. He answered yes when asked whether he had paid Cantu to kill Tricia Cummings. He answered yes when asked whether Cantu told him that he had killed the wrong person. He answered yes when asked whether Cantu had left a gun at the scene in order to make it appear that Dorris Quaker had murdered her children and then committed suicide. When I finished telling her about the questions and answers, she said, And? I told her that Faison would have a complete report later, but it was his opinion that Green was being truthful on all the questions. She said, I am not going to say I told you so.

I said, Why not?

She said, Because I'm starving, and I want you to bring my steak in here to me.

■   ■   ■

As I WAS PACKING my bag the next morning Lincoln said, Why do you have to leave today, Dada? I told him that I needed to try to help someone. He said, But it's probably not going to work, right?

I wondered whether he had heard me say that, or deduced it himself. He said, Won't the person die anyway? I said yes, but that I still thought I needed to help him. He said, That doesn't make any sense. Besides, why can't his mom or dad help him?

I said, Amigo, he doesn't have anyone who can help him. You and I are very lucky. We have lots of people who love us and who would try to help us if we were in trouble. This man I am trying to help doesn't have anyone. I think it's important to try to help people who don't have anyone. Don't you?

He was quiet for a minute. I asked him whether everything was okay. He said, Yes, I'm just thinking. I touched his cheek. He said, Dada, I'm glad you are trying to help that person, but I still wish you were staying with Mama and me for a little while longer.

■　■　■

O'NEILL HAD BEEN PLACED in mental hospitals more than a dozen times, usually by his parents, a couple of times by the courts. In a layperson's terms, he was crazy. But being crazy matters in different ways at different phases of the criminal justice system. At a trial, if a defendant is too mentally ill to aid his lawyers, then he is incompetent to stand trial, and so the government keeps him in a mental institution until he is capable of standing trial or dies, whichever comes first. If, following a trial, a jury finds that the defendant did not know the difference between right and wrong, then he is criminally insane, and he can't be sent to prison, but he can be sent to a mental institution, until he is healed or dies, whichever comes first. If a defendant is not found insane and is sentenced to death, but he becomes crazy while on death row, then the state cannot execute him, so the person stays crazy in prison until he dies, or the state medicates him so he is not crazy anymore, and then they can kill him. Contrary to conventional mythology, being crazy is not a get-out-of-jail-free card, and life in the cuckoo's nest isn't all that different from life in the joint.

The problem we had in O'Neill's case, though, is that in 1996 Congress passed a law that basically makes it impossible for death-row inmates to challenge their convictions in federal court more than one time. When O'Neill went to federal court the first time, his lawyers did not say he was incompetent to be executed, because his execution was still years away. In addition to that, he had gotten worse and worse over the years. He might not have been incompetent to be executed when he first arrived on death row, but he certainly was now. We had already been to federal court, however, and we were not being successful in persuading the courts that they should allow us to come back. We were pinning our hopes on an obscure Supreme Court case that seemed to create an exception to the law for people who were raising issues that did not previously exist. The lower federal court was not persuaded, and we did not have much confidence that the court of appeals would be persuaded, either, but if the court of appeals wanted our appeal by Saturday afternoon, that meant they would probably rule against us first thing Monday morning, and we would have all day to get to the Supreme Court.

Everyone was at the office when I got there. Most lawyers have the philosophy that they should try to win in whatever forum they happen to be. So if you are in the trial court, think about winning there, not in the court of appeals. If you are in the court of appeals, think about winning there, not in the Supreme Court. The problem with that approach for death-penalty lawyers in Texas is that the federal court of appeals with jurisdiction over our clients consists mostly of judges who are utterly unprincipled and hostile to the rule of law. They look for ways to uphold death sentences even where constitutional violations are egregious. In recent years, the court upheld a death sentence of a black inmate who was sentenced to death by an all-white jury after prosecutors systematically removed every potential juror of color from serving. It upheld the death sentence of a mentally retarded inmate after his lawyer, who was afflicted by Parkinson's disease, neglected to point out the inmate's IQ score. It upheld the death sentence of an inmate who was probably innocent on the ground that his lawyers had waited too long to identify the proof of innocence. It upheld the death sentence of an inmate whose lawyer had literally slept through the trial. These judges get to be judges not because they are wise, but because they are friends with their U.S. senator, or a friend of a friend. They are smart, however. That means they are very good at hiding their lawlessness inside of recondite-sounding legalese. They look for reasons to ensure that a death-row inmate will get executed, and they usually find one. And not very many people care. Do you care that the rights of some murderer were violated? Most people say that the murderer got treated better than his victim, and that pretty much sums up the attitude of the judges on the court of appeals as well.

Justices on the Supreme Court are slightly better. They could hardly be worse. But the big problem with counting on winning a victory in the Supreme Court is that the justices are so inundated with cases that they don't have time to be sticklers for principle, even when they are so inclined. Nevertheless, even an infinitesimally small chance of victory is infinitely greater than a zero chance. I told Jerome that we should write something cursory for the court of appeals, since we knew we were going to lose, and start working on writing a powerful appeal to the Supreme Court. Gary disagreed. He reminded me that the Supreme Court had recently agreed to hear a case from Alabama called *Nelson*, and that the issue in *Nelson* was very similar to the issue we were raising in *O'Neill*. Maybe, he suggested, we could ask the court of appeals to postpone O'Neill's execution until the Supreme Court decided the *Nelson* case. I did not think it would work, but it did make sense. I opted for sensibility over probability. We wrote an appeal pointing out that even though the court of appeals had ruled against us in other cases raising a similar issue, the court should act differently in this case in view of the Supreme Court's obvious interest in this issue. For good measure, we reminded the court how mentally disturbed O'Neill was. We sent the appeal to the court by e-mail at a quarter to five.

■   ■   ■

SUNDAY MORNING Fred Faison called to let me know that he had dropped off his report at my office. I asked him for the Cliffs Notes version. He said, Anyone who trusts these machines will not find any deception in Mr. Green's answers. I asked him what his report said. He said, It says that, in my opinion, Mr. Green's claims of knowledge and responsibility for the murders of the Quaker family are truthful.

I said, So you are saying that you believe my client is innocent.

He said, I'm saying that I believe what Green said.

Two days later we had polygraphed Quaker. I had not been there. Faison said he was telling the truth, too.

Mark Roberts lived in my neighborhood. I e-mailed him and asked whether he had time to chat later that day. He called me a few minutes later and asked whether I'd had breakfast. I told him I hadn't. He said, Let's ride our bikes to the Breakfast Klub and talk there. Roberts had been a semiprofessional cyclist before he gave it up and went to law school. I told him I wasn't sure he could pedal slow enough for me to keep up. He said, I just finished a seventy-miler. I was about to jump into the shower. You'll be able to keep up.

We both ordered waffles and wings. I told him our problems. There was blood from a victim in Quaker's car. He had life insurance on his family. He was mentally unbalanced from the fire. A gun he owned had disappeared. Cantu was gone, and it probably wouldn't matter even if he weren't. Unless he was on death row somewhere, so that he didn't have anything to lose, I didn't see him clearing his conscience to save

163

a guy he didn't know. Kassie had found Tricia Cummings, the woman Green had supposedly wanted Cantu to kill. She had gotten married, changed her name to Tricia Davis, had a daughter, and died of a heroin overdose. She was buried in the Fourth Ward. That pretty much left us nothing but Green's statement.

Roberts said, How did they convict the guy with just that?

He was right, of course. Daniel had frequent nosebleeds. Quaker had told me that, and the nurse at Daniel's school verified it. The blood meant nothing. The life insurance also proved very little. The insurance agent gave Gary a statement that she had pressured Henry to buy it when he came to see her to buy auto insurance. It hadn't even been his idea, and either he forgot he had it or had no interest in it after the murders, because he took no steps to collect the money. I said, His lawyer was Jack Gatling. Roberts nodded and chewed on a wing.

He said, Listen, I'm sympathetic, but I think I've done everything I can at this point. I have a call arranged with Green for Tuesday. I'll tell him that you and I have talked. I already said you can use his statement if he doesn't make it to Friday, but if we catch lightning in a bottle, I don't see how I can agree. He'll be opening himself up to another death sentence. I'll tell him that, and if he wants to fire me if he gets a commutation so that he can talk to you, then he can.

I asked Roberts whether it was okay with him if I tried to talk to Green one more time on Thursday. He said, You mean while he's in the holding cell? I nodded. He said, What? You figure he'll be like Honest Abe thirty minutes before he gets the juice?

I said, You never know.

He said, This is why I don't want my clients to be innocent. Too much pressure.

I ate the last bite of my waffle and said, Do we have to ride back home or can we call a cab? He laughed, which I took to mean we were riding.

■ ■ ■

Jᴇʀᴏᴍᴇ sᴘᴇɴᴛ ᴛʜᴇ ɴɪɢʜᴛ at the office on Sunday. When I got there just after seven on Monday morning, he was asleep on my sofa. I said, Hey, Little Red Riding Hood, you want some coffee? He sat up and apologized. He washed his face and came back into my office with the appeal for the Supreme Court he had spent the night writing. It was seventy pages. I said, This is too long. We've got to chop it down.

He said, I know.

I said, Good thing we have eleven hours.

Considering that the court of appeals had had our petition since late Saturday afternoon, and considering that law clerks work long hours on weekends even though their judicial bosses do not, I expected that we were going to hear something from the court first thing in the morning. When neither fax nor e-mail had arrived by ten, I asked Jerome to call the clerk, just to make sure they had not sent something that hadn't reached us. She said that the court had not yet announced a decision. Gary and Kassie went next door to pick up Vietnamese food.

165

I sat at my computer, trying to work on the Quaker case, but I couldn't concentrate on it, so I buzzed Jerome on the intercom and told him I'd take over editing the O'Neill appeal. He said he was almost finished, that it was down to fifty pages, exactly what is allowed. So I sat in my chair, bounced the Super Ball against the wall, and downloaded an Art Tatum song from iTunes.

Kassie walked in and said, We're eating in the conference room. My fortune says that all great battles are lost in the middle. I think it's Lao Tzu. Do you think middle refers to the court of appeals? She smiled.

I said, I heard it as all great wars. I thought you were going to the Vietnamese place.

She said, We did.

I said, I don't think you can place much faith in a fortune cookie from a Vietnamese joint.

She said, I think that might be a racist comment.

At two o'clock the clerk called and told us the court had issued its opinion. They had e-mailed it to me. She asked whether I wanted a copy in the mail. I laughed. No thank you, I said. The four of us stood in a semicircle, reading the pages as they came off the printer. We had lost, but we had lost in a very surprising way. There are eighteen judges on the court of appeals, but they sit in panels of three to decide cases. The rule on the court is that once a panel decides an issue a certain way, all the judges on the court, even if they were not on that panel, are required to decide the same issue in the same way, unless the court as a whole reverses the panel decision. The panel that decided our case seemed to have agreed with Gary's argument that they should hold the case until the Supreme Court ruled in *Nelson*. But, according to the judges, a previous panel had decided a similar issue already, and so our panel was not at liberty to grant us the relief we were asking for.

As I read the panel's opinion, the judges were almost inviting us to ask the entire court to review the case. I said to the others, Does it seem to you all that they are asking us to request en banc reconsideration? We all pored over the opinion again.

Gary said, If the panel does want us to request en banc reconsideration, and we don't, how will that look when we appeal to the Supremes?

I didn't think our chances in the Supreme Court would be much affected one way or the other. At the same time, if we were right that the panel was nudging us to request that the full court of appeals address the issue, then maybe they had some inkling that the full court would grant our request. Otherwise, why propose a tactic that would just consume valuable time? I said, En banc reconsideration it is. We briefly discussed how to frame the argument. Gary and Kassie went with Jerome into his office, and an hour later they handed me a motion. I read it quickly, made a minor change or two, and said, File it.

Our motion for en banc reconsideration got to the court at three thirty. The clerk called us to confirm receipt. O'Neill was sitting in a van, on his way from the Polunsky Unit in Livingston, where death-row inmates are housed, to the Walls Unit in Huntsville, where they are killed. His execution was two and a half hours away.

▦   ▦   ▦

JEROME LEFT for the prison. He would deliver the news to O'Neill that we had lost, and then watch our client get executed. Kassie asked him whether he wanted her to go with him and drive. He thanked her and said no. He called at five, just as he was about to go visit with O'Neill in the holding cell. He wanted to know whether there was any news. I said there wasn't. He said, That's good, right? They would have denied us by now if they were going to deny us, don't you think?

Being a death-penalty lawyer requires constant delusion. You have to convince yourself that even though you hardly ever win, this time is going to be different. I said, Don't get his hopes up.

Jerome said, I don't think it makes one bit of difference what I say to this guy.

He had me there. I said, Well, if you see his parents, don't get their hopes up.

Fifteen years ago, before they changed it to 6:00 p.m. so that the guards could be home in time for dinner, Texas carried out executions at midnight. The death warrant instructed the warden to carry out the execution on a certain date, before sunrise. So the execution window lasted roughly six hours, from midnight until dawn. We represented an inmate named Lupe Hernandez. The day before his execution, the widow of Hernandez's brother showed us a letter in which the brother claimed credit for the murder that our client was going to be executed for. We filed a last-minute appeal, on the day of the execution. After a flurry of skirmishes in the lower courts, we got to the Supreme Court around nine o'clock at night. At nearly five in the morning, there was still no word from the justices. Dawn would soon break over East Texas, and the death warrant would expire. At a quarter past five, a state court judge stayed the execution, with an opinion saying that the State of Texas should not carry out an execution while the highest court in the land was still considering the appeal.

But inherent in that state court judge's opinion was a point that gave me a chill as we waited for the court of appeals to issue a ruling in the O'Neill case: Unless a court or the governor granted a stay of execution, the warden could carry out the execution at any time between six and midnight. The fact that we had filed an appeal meant nothing. We needed the court to tell the warden that he could not go forward.

At seven thirty there was still no word. Jerome had called half a dozen times, thinking that his cell phone must not be ringing. Each time I told him that the court had not called. In the office, we grew more hopeful. There would be no reason to take so long, if the court was simply going to issue its form-letter denial of our request.

The phone rang at a quarter past eight. The clerk of the court and a lawyer from the attorney general's office were on the line. The clerk said, I am calling to let you know that the court has instructed me that it will be taking no further action tonight.

What? There were nearly four hours left in the execution window. We had gotten our appeal to the court five hours before. The judges had had plenty of time. How could they go home? I said, When will they make a decision?

The clerk said, The court has instructed me that it will be taking no further action tonight.

I said, Can we file a motion with the panel asking them to grant a stay until the entire court has an opportunity to rule on our motion?

The clerk said, The court has instructed me that it will be taking no further action tonight.

You have to beat me upside the head only so many times. I said okay and told the clerk good-bye, then told the assistant attorney general that I would call her right back. Gary said, I think we need to file in the Supreme Court.

Kassie disagreed, saying we did not need to do anything. She said, They can't kill him with our motion still pending.

I was not so sure about that. We called the attorney general's office. The lawyer handling the case was an experienced death-penalty lawyer named Eddy Martin. She said, I've spoken to my boss and the attorney general. We are going to advise our client not to go forward with the execution this evening.

I said, Eddy, can you assure us that the warden will follow your advice?

She said, No, I cannot.

I said, We'll call you back.

I called Jerome and explained to him what had happened. I said, I need you to talk to the warden, or someone in his office, and find out whether he is going to follow Eddy's recommendation.

Ten minutes later he called back. He said, The warden's assistant was very nice. She said that the warden wouldn't talk to me.

If death-penalty lawyers made a lot of money, this is where they would earn it. It was around nine. There were three hours left during which the warden could lawfully execute O'Neill. The attorney general's office had told the warden not to go through with it, but we did not know whether the warden would listen. After all, he was holding a court order commanding him to carry out the execution. We had two options. One was to do nothing and hope the warden listened to a lawyer's advice rather than adhering to a judicial order. I figured there was a fifty-fifty chance he would. The other was to file a motion with the Supreme Court and ask that Court to stay the execution. There were a couple of problems with the latter approach. One was an arcane legal problem having to do with on what basis we would ask the Supreme Court to intervene. Typically, when someone asks the Supreme Court to do something, the party making the request argues that the lower court got the wrong answer to the question. In our case, the lower court had not gotten the wrong answer; it hadn't given an answer. There was, therefore, nothing to appeal from. Although I felt we could overcome that issue, the other problem was more pragmatic: If the Supreme Court refused to intervene, maybe the warden would interpret that refusal as authorization to proceed. I figured we had slightly under a fifty-fifty chance of getting a stay from the Court.

Call heads or tails, I said to Gary. Let's just decide by flipping a coin. He and Kassie stared at me. I said, I'm kidding.

We decided to do nothing. I called Jerome to let him know. He said, What? Y'all are just going to sit there? I said that was the plan. He said, You want me to tell his parents? I told him

171

that I would call them. I was not doing it just to be nice. I was doing it so that I had something to do.

I filled a coffee mug with crushed ice and took it and a bottle of Jack Daniel's and climbed out my window onto the fire escape. I called Katya and told her what was up. When I told her about the judges on the court of appeals calling it a day while our motion was still pending, she said, You need to file a judicial grievance. I told her I didn't see what good it would do. She said, That's not the point. You need to hold their feet to the fire. That is inexcusable. They shouldn't be allowed to get away with not justifying themselves.

I said, K, you've got a lot of spunk. But she wasn't in a smiling mood. I told her I'd call when something, or nothing, happened.

At ten minutes past midnight, Jerome called. They're taking him back to Polunsky, he said. Jerome told me that the warden had called him just before midnight to ask him whether he wanted to say anything to O'Neill before they drove him back. Jerome went back to see O'Neill in the holding cell. O'Neill had ordered a half a gallon of vanilla ice cream as his final meal. It was served to him when he got to the Walls Unit at four that afternoon. When Jerome went to see him, O'Neill was drinking the vanilla ice cream with a spoon, like it was soup. Jerome repeated to me what O'Neill said: Tell that gentleman that you work with that I told him not to concern himself. His wings and his breath surround me. Please tell him I thank him for his efforts all the same. Will you kindly ask whether I can bring this ice cream back with me?

■   ■   ■

*W*ON AND *ONE* are homophones, spelled differently but pronounced the same, like *two* and *too*. My wife, on the other hand, says *Juan* when she means *won*, and she says it like a Mexican. I make fun of this habit. When she asks how things went at Lincoln's Little League games, I say, It was great. Both teams *Juan.* Lincoln always corrects me. (My pronunciation, that is, not my content. It is t-ball. Both teams did win.) Before I walked down to my car, I sent her a text. It read, *Oui Juan.* She called as I was driving home. I asked her what she was still doing up. She said, Waiting for you to call me. I told her the story.

Lincoln was getting bored in Galveston. I told Katya that the two of them should come back to Houston for a few days. She asked whether I had a Plan B. This was a reasonable question. In the midst of futilely trying to save a client, I've been an asshole twenty or thirty times too many. I'm short-tempered and surly and altogether unpleasant to be around. Having client after client get killed can do that to you. But I was not going to be working on the Green case, and I was not yet feeling desperate about Quaker.

I said, I promise not to be entirely impossible.

She said, Pretty tall order, cowboy, but she still agreed they'd stay the week and leave the following weekend.

I was going to be driving to the prison first thing the next morning to see Quaker, so I decided to get some groceries on my way home. At one in the morning, you pretty much have the supermarket to yourself. The only other person in the produce section was a tall, lean, Marlboro-looking middle-aged man wearing a belt buckle the size of a cantaloupe and brown lizard-skin boots. He squinted at me while he filled a plastic bag with fat jalapeño peppers. Did I know him? He was too old to have been a student of mine. He walked over and said, Did I see you on the news tonight? I told him I wasn't sure. He said, Wasn't you one of the lawyers fighting for that retarded man?

There is always a point in my conversations with strangers where I have to decide whether to lie. This time I didn't. I told him that I was.

I'm accustomed to what was coming. Whenever my name is in the paper, I get a dozen e-mails telling me my client is a worthless pig, and I'm even worse. (Sadly, most venomous e-mails tend to lack much creativity.) But here's the thing about living in Texas: It's a big state. The man with the peppers shook my hand like we were old friends. He said, My papa was shot in front of me when I was eleven years old. It happened right there in the kitchen. He was drinking a cup of tea. When I joined a group to fight against the death penalty, it just about tore my sister up. She doesn't understand it at all, but I just don't think we oughta be doing it. I told her, After you kill the bad guys, you're just as angry as you were before, but there ain't no one left to hate.

He was still holding my hand. He looked down like he'd forgotten about it, then he looked embarrassed and let me go and shoved his hands deep into his back pockets. He said, I didn't mean to take up so much of your time. I just wanted to say I admire what you do.

■   ■   ■

WHEN I GOT HOME, I fixed a turkey sandwich and carried it and a bottle of Shiner beer up to my room. The ten o'clock news was repeating, and they showed the picture of me that the man in the grocery store must have seen. The video had been shot in the morning, when we were working on the papers we thought we would file in the Supreme Court. The scene was fourteen hours old. I could barely remember it, like it was something that had happened years ago. People sometimes think I am younger than I am, because my hair is short and not too gray, and all I wear is blue jeans. But I noticed my hands gesturing for the reporter. Hands always reveal age. The skin was thin and papery, dotted with sun spots. Through the wrinkles you could see the veins, thick and green. I looked at my fingers and thought, This is pointless. Then I thought, I've been doing this too long.

There is a relationship between those two ideas that I know to be true but that I will not acknowledge. There are certain truths in life you have to evade in order to keep being the person you have convinced yourself that you are.

■   ■   ■

BEING AT THE PRISON the day after staving off an execution is the closest I come to being a rock star. Inmates sitting in their cages look at you as if you're magical. Chaplains and nuns, holding the tattered Bibles that they read to murderers, greet you as if you're Joshua. Parents and spouses and children of the inmates stare at you the way Auschwitz survivors stared at the Allied soldiers who came to liberate them. It makes me want to slink out and never return. Most blind squirrels starve. When you see one find an acorn, you can easily forget that.

Quaker told me that he had dreamed about his family the night before. He was in a pit with smooth sides. He tried to climb out, but there was no way to get any traction. He sank down to the floor, shirt soaked with sweat, wondering where he was, and why. He looked up, and Daniel was peeking down at him from over the edge. His first instinct was to shout at Daniel to get away from the edge so he wouldn't fall. Then he felt lightness and love, like he could float. Daniel dropped him a pair of platform shoes. Wearing them, he could press his feet against one wall and reach out to the other with his arms. In this fashion, he crawled up the sides of the pit. As he emerged, he saw Charisse, hiding playfully behind Daniel. He hugged them both and realized he was crying. He lifted his head and saw Dorris, wearing just a negligee, sitting in a bed. She said, Daniel, Charisse, can you two run off to your rooms for a little while and leave Daddy and me alone? Henry took a step toward her. He smelled her perfume. He woke up as the guard banged open the slot in the steel cell door and passed him breakfast.

He said, It was the best night I've had in years. We sat quietly for nearly a minute, then he added, I heard yours was pretty good, too.

I told him about the last-minute activity in the O'Neill case, and then I told him again about our plan for the hearing. But I had a bad feeling I had used up all my luck. Maybe he read my mind. He said, You remember that story I told you about when I was in the psych hospital in New Braunfels after the fire? I said I did. He said, I feel like that right now, man. My will is spent. I ain't gonna tell you to give up or to stop what you're doing, but if we lose, it's okay. It really is. I'm ready to just be done with it, you know what I mean?

I knew exactly what he meant, but I didn't say so. Instead I said, I'm not planning for us to lose.

■   ■   ▓

WHEN I GOT HOME, Katya and Lincoln were there, playing a video game that I did not understand. Lincoln shouted, Dada, and came running to me. I kissed Katya and she hugged me tight, squeezing the air out of me.

I said, Hey, be gentle with me, and Lincoln laughed.

He went to the closet under the stairs and came back with our baseball gloves and a tennis ball. He said, Dada, can we play catch? I looked at Katya and she nodded. She said she'd go pick up Thai food while we were playing.

The temperature had dropped into the upper forties, which in Houston is cold enough to justify a fire in the fireplace. Lincoln and I carried in some logs, and Katya put the take-out cartons on the coffee table in the library. I said, Hey Linco, do you want to try this chicken with basil and peppers?

He said, In case you forgot, Dada, I'm a vegetarian. I told him I had not forgotten, that I was only kidding around. He said, Oh. Well, it's not very funny. You shouldn't kill animals to eat them.

Katya said, What a guy.

I said, I know it.

And I thought to myself, I wonder if I disappoint him.

■ ■ ■

FOR THE NEXT TWO DAYS, I went to my office at five so I could be home by eleven or twelve. Katya, Lincoln, and I rode our bikes, sat by the fire and watched *SpongeBob*, read books, went out to lunch, played board games, tossed the tennis ball, and saw some movies. On Thursday morning, as we were finishing our pancakes, Lincoln said, What are we going to do when you get home today, Dada? It was the day of Green's execution. I told him that he was going to have to hang out with Mama today, because I had to go to the prison. He said, Are you trying to help some person? I told him that someone else was trying to help the man. I was just going to go visit him. He said, Why can't you help him, too?

It had been hard enough explaining to Lincoln that I try to help people who have killed somebody. It would be harder to explain that, in truth, I can't really help anybody. Last summer, Gary, Kassie, and I spent a week in East Texas, in the Arnold Broxton case. The only issue in the trial was whether Broxton is mentally retarded. There was no jury. A judge would decide. With an impartial adjudicator, it would have been a close call.

Of course, with an impartial adjudicator, we would have been somewhere besides East Texas.

Broxton's IQ scores were right on the border of mental retardation, so the critical factor was whether we could produce evidence of what are called adaptive behavior deficits. People with mild mental retardation can live independent and productive lives, but they have limitations that result from their mental health. They cannot do certain things, like attend to their hygiene, hold a job, maintain a home, and the like. Lawyers prove that their mentally retarded clients have these adaptive deficits by calling witnesses who have known the inmate for a long time and can testify as to these limitations.

Broxton has a younger brother. He would be our key witness on adaptive deficits. He had seen his older brother fail and fail again. He had worked with Broxton at a flooring company and he recounted, among other things, that Broxton could simply never learn how to lay tile. In the days leading up to the trial, Broxton and his brother had several telephone conversations. The sheriff's office recorded them. At the trial, the state planned to use the recordings to prove that Broxton was aware of what was happening in his case and was therefore not mentally retarded.

Now this argument is as moronic as it is a non sequitur. Mentally retarded inmates can often understand what their lawyers tell them, and we had told Broxton what the hearing was about, and how we were going to proceed. But that's not the point of this story. Broxton and his brother had spent pretty much all their lives either in inner-city housing projects or in prison. Their idiom reflected that history. The language in their conversations was R-rated and coarse. Every other word was *nigger*-this or *nigger*-

that. Broxton had been convicted of murdering a convenience store clerk; it was not a high-profile or an infamous crime, but we were in a small town, where every murder trial is a big deal, especially when the defendant is black. East Texas timber country is still a Klan-friendly place.

The local TV news stations were filming the proceedings from beginning to end. The lawyer for the state was the elected district attorney, and he was putting on a show. He played a CD-ROM of the conversations between the two Broxton brothers. The conversations had been transcribed. He handed me a copy of the transcript, and read aloud several lines of dialogue. He did so, mimicking the patois of the Broxton brothers. Even by East Texas standards, it was appalling. I stood up and said, Excuse me, Judge. I would like the record to reflect that the district attorney is no longer speaking in his natural voice, but is trying to sound like my client and his brother. The fact that he is failing miserably at sounding like either one of them does not make his effort any less offensive.

The judge had been checking her e-mail or playing Solitaire or doing something on her computer, and she looked up, baffled. She said, Is that an objection?

I said, Not really. It is a simple expression of moral outrage.

She stared at me and said, Treating it as an objection, the objection is overruled.

The district attorney smirked. He immediately resumed his effort to sound like a brother. I started to rise from my seat again. Gary gently put his hand on my arm and, in a whisper, told me to count to ten. I said, I'm already up to thirty-seven and it isn't helping.

This is the reality: When you know that you are not going to succeed, and that your client is going to die no matter what you do, and that it does not matter a whit whether the facts and the law are on your side, you can either do nothing and accept defeat, or modify your definition of success, but what you also have to realize is that even if you choose the latter route and opt to redefine the meaning of winning, and therefore count it as a small victory (for example) when you don't sit silently by while a district attorney puts on his black face and carries on for the cameras with an egregious display of overt racism, your client is still going to get escorted into the execution chamber, strapped down to the gurney, and put to death.

There are some philosophers who say that we create the world we live in with our language. I am sorry to say that that is not how it works. Reality is a relentless and crushing force, and it cannot be thwarted or outrun with a lawyer's effete semantics.

I told Lincoln that I'd try to help the person I was going to see, and I headed for the prison.

▓ ▓ ▓

AN ALABAMA SONG was playing on the radio. It reminded me of when I had picked up Lincoln from Rachel's house after a playdate six months before. Alabama was singing about how angels come down from heaven to visit us when we're sad. Lincoln asked me to play it again. I told him I couldn't because it had been on the radio. He downloaded it from iTunes as soon

181

as we got home and sat in front of his computer listening to it, over and over. When Katya called him to dinner he said, This song brings tears to my eyes.

I'd never seen him so morose. Katya gently pressed him to tell us why he was sad. He said, It's because I don't have any courage.

Yes you do, amigo. You have plenty of courage.

It's not true.

His lower lip trembled like he was about to start crying. But he didn't. Katya said, Lincoln, why do you think you don't have any courage?

He said, Rachel was sad. I don't know why. I could tell she was sad, and I didn't have the courage to say anything to her.

Katya said, Sometimes it's hard to talk to someone who's sad, isn't it?

Yeah.

Well, Lincoln, no matter what you say, if you are trying to make that person feel better, she will appreciate it. Do you understand what I mean?

Yeah. Thanks, Mama.

■   ■   ■

THE HOLDING CELL has a distinctly medieval feel. It is damp and dark and gray. There is no TV or radio, but there is a rotary-dial telephone on the concrete floor that might have been new in the 1970s. To get to the place where condemned prisoners spend the final three hours of their lives, you pass through two electronically controlled doors. Then you exit the prison through a heavy steel door that opens with a key that is eight inches long. The warden's assistant, the key dangling from her neck as if she were a character in a Dickens novel, escorted me across a small courtyard, really just a rectangle of grass surrounded by concrete walls, and knocked on another door like the one through which we just passed. A guard inside peered through a slot covered with Plexiglas and visually identified my escort and me. Then he opened the door with another giant key. The warden's assistant left, and I was standing in an L-shaped, windowless area.

The base of the L is the actual holding cell; the rest is a short hall where the three guards stood and watched over Green. To my right, as I faced Green, was another steel door that looks like it belongs on a submarine. It is the entrance to the room where inmates die. The holding cell itself has two walls of cinder block, and two walls of steel bars covered with a mesh that looks like chicken wire. A metal cot is bolted to one wall, and there is a stainless-steel toilet. It is five steps long and two and a half steps wide.

Green was sitting on the cot, inhaling through his nose and exhaling loudly through his mouth. Beads of sweat covered his forehead and his upper lip. For a brief moment I thought he had not heard me come in. The three guards lingered off to my left standing next to a small table, talking in low voices that were not quite a whisper. On the table was a plate piled with french fries and a second plate with a slice of pie covered with whipped cream from a can. There was a squeeze bottle of Hunt's ketchup and a plastic cup with what looked like lemonade. Green looked at me and said, Hey. Just then the phone rang. A guard picked it up, spoke briefly, and handed it to Green. Green said, Uh-huh, uh-huh, okay, and handed the receiver back to the guard. He said to me, That was Mr. Roberts. I got turned down.

When my clients ask me to, I watch them die. When they don't, I sit in my office until the courts and the governor's office have all turned down our final requests for relief, then I close my door and call my client, just like Mark Roberts had just done. I make notes to remind myself not to say certain things, like Talk to you later, or Take care, or See you around, or any of the other meaningless expressions that pepper our everyday discourse and that become suddenly full of meaning when they aren't true and can't possibly be. I found myself standing next to Green with no Post-its to remind me what not to say and no script of what I wanted to cover. I said, I'm sorry. Green leaned forward and held his head in his hands. I wanted to be outside. I said, I just wanted to come see you to say thanks for trying to help me.

He said, All right.

I had no idea why I was there. Did I expect Green to say he had been making it up? Or maybe I hoped he'd reveal some proof that he wasn't. What was I thinking? I got the attention of one of the guards and nodded toward the door. I said to Green, You have any messages or anything you want me to pass on to anyone?

He said, My old man used to beat me with a switch. Made it from a peach tree we had in the yard. He said he liked to use peach wood 'cause it left big ol' welts. Mr. Roberts asked him how come he didn't never beat me with his fist. He said 'cause he didn't want to hurt his hands.

The guard put the giant key in the lock. Green said, Everything I done tol' you is the truth. I swear to God.

There's an old joke among death-penalty lawyers. Once you've killed somebody, swearing to tell the truth, so help you God, doesn't pack quite the same punch it did before. I said, I appreciate it.

He said, Henry Quaker didn't kill nobody. I know that for a fact.

I said, Thanks again, Green. I'll see you down the road. He didn't look up.

The guard opened the door, and I walked out into the twilight chill.

■   ■   ■

A SMALL GROUP of death-penalty opponents stood outside the prison, twenty or twenty-five people in all, a few black, the rest white. Each person held a small candle. Some had posters with the usual clichés: Why Do We Kill People for Killing People to Show That Killing Is Wrong? Et cetera. I nodded at several I knew. Brigitte walked over and asked whether I was representing Green. I said no. She asked whether I thought he would get a stay, and I told her they were moving him from the holding cell to the execution chamber at that very moment. She works in the French consulate's office and is genuinely perplexed by the death penalty. She squeezed my forearm and said, This is terrible. Will you come stand with us?

Protesting against the death penalty in Texas takes a certain passion I do not have, or maybe what I lack is courage. The fraternity boys at the university across the street heckle the demonstrators and occasionally throw bananas and paper cups filled with warm beer. Sheriff's deputies ticket their cars and threaten to arrest them if they chant too loudly or get too close to the yellow tape. My friend Dave Atwood spent the night in the Walker County jail after someone jostled him and his right foot momentarily crossed the police barricade. I stood several feet behind them, not part of them, feeling alienated, I suppose, and watched the minute hand of the clock on the prison tower slide toward six. At nineteen minutes past, the prison spokesperson came out. She reported that Green shook his head no when asked if he had a final statement, that he glanced briefly at his wife, and then stared at the ceiling as the injection began. He coughed twice, and was pronounced dead at 6:11 p.m. Another witness who covers executions for the local paper stood at the podium next. He said that the reporters could see bruises on Green's arm and could hear Green saying, This is torture, before he lost consciousness. As another reporter stepped up to the lectern, I got in my car and drove off.

When I walked in Katya was in the kitchen. She asked how it went. I shook my head and asked her to tell me about her day instead. I went upstairs and kissed our sleeping son. I threw my clothes in the machine and got in the shower. When I came back downstairs, Katya was tossing a salad and heating up leftover red beans and rice in the microwave. Most death-

penalty lawyers I know are married to other death-penalty lawyers. I'm glad I'm not. I am opposed to death. I want to come
home and be far away from it. I asked Katya whether she had
TiVo-ed *American Idol*. I said, Let's carry our plates in and watch,
okay?

She held my head in her hands, each hand cupping an ear.
She kissed me and said, Sounds good to me.

■   ■   ■

IN MY DREAM I thought I heard a noise. I went downstairs
to investigate. The wind had blown open the kitchen door.
I drank a quart of water from the refrigerator, and the light
blinded me. When I turned to go back upstairs I tripped over
Lincoln's stool. I'd told him dozens of times to put it away. I
went upstairs and woke him up. It was nearly 3:00 a.m., and
he had been sleeping deeply. He looked at me and then at the
clock and said, Huh? I made him follow me into the kitchen. I
asked him why he thought I had brought him there. He said he
didn't know. I asked him again. I told him he was a smart boy
and he could figure it out. I waited. He said he didn't know, and
he started to cry.

I said, You left the goddam stool out again. I could have
tripped and broken my neck.

He said, I'm sorry, Dada.

I said, Put it away.

He started to push it into the closet but a wheel had come

off and it would not roll. He tried to pick it up, but it was heavy and unwieldy and he dropped it. It landed on my foot and sliced open my big toe. I said, Shit, and slumped to the ground. I grabbed some ice and wrapped it in a towel. Lincoln asked whether I was okay and I said no, but he didn't seem concerned. I told him that it hurt a lot. He rubbed his eyes and said he was sorry. But he didn't mean it.

I wanted real remorse from him. I stood up so I would tower over him. I raised my voice. I said he had really hurt my foot. I told him to look at me when I was talking to him. I said that when you hurt someone you have to apologize. I said that when you apologize you have to mean it. I said that I know that accidents happen but you need to take precautions to try to avoid them. I told him that he needed to be more careful, that he needed to put away his things, that when he hurt someone he needed to be sincere.

I was relentless. I wanted him to feel bad. I wanted him to cry. I knew at that point that it was a dream and that I was out of control, and I tried to make myself wake up, but I couldn't. It was like a fat man was sitting on my chest. I was straining not to scream. I had that crazed, talking-through-one's-teeth tone that people have when they've lost it but are trying to sound like they haven't. But I couldn't be kind.

He burst into tears. I had never understood that expression, but that's what happened. He exploded with crying. His whole body was shaking. He was trying to control himself, to use the measured breathing we had practiced, and he couldn't. He was shaking his hands, the way you would shake them in the cold to make them warm. He was saying, Dada, Dada, Dada. Again

I struggled to wake myself up. I felt a fissure crack open inside my belly and a sensation like steam pouring out and I sagged to the ground. I hugged him. I told him that I knew he hadn't done it on purpose. I kept saying that I knew it was an accident. I felt his tears on my cheek, but maybe they were my own. I squeezed him tighter, afraid it was too tight, and said that I knew he would not hurt me on purpose. I said, I just want you to be more careful, pal, that's all. I'm sorry I shouted at you. He did not say anything. He wrapped his arms around my neck, like he was saving himself from drowning in my anger. I said to him, I'm sorry, Lincoln. I'm sorry. I'm sorry, sweet boy.

I felt him relax. I felt him trust me. I said, Hey how about if I hurt you to make it even? He said okay. I asked him to get me a hammer. We both started laughing.

Katya appeared. She said, What's going on?

I said, I thought I heard something in the kitchen.

I bolted upright. I was clasping my pillow so hard that my arms were sore. In the distance I could hear a train whistle. Katya was sound asleep. I walked into Lincoln's room and sat on the edge of his bed. I watched his eyelids flutter and his lips twitch.

I feel like I understand some crimes and criminals. I could kill someone who killed someone I love. I could rob or steal. But I've never understood people who can hurt children. Knowing how they get to be who they are is not the same as understanding.

I kissed Lincoln's forehead and touched his cheek. I watched him sleep. At the parent-teacher conference we had gone to a month before, his teacher, who's been teaching thirty years, said to us, Lincoln is possibly the happiest child I have ever met.

She could have told us that he was smarter than Einstein and it wouldn't have been as good.

I asked myself, How can I not spoil this beautiful boy's happiness?

Katya came in and asked me what was wrong. I said, I broke my promise, and I was also a shitty dad. I told her about the dream.

She said, You're kidding, right?

No, I'm not.

It was a dream. That doesn't count. And anyway, even in the dream, you weren't shitty. Maybe a little harsh, but not shitty. You're not shitty just because you're not always perfect. And as per usual, you melted as soon as he started crying.

I said, So you're saying that I was harsh and imperfect up until I hugged him?

She said, Yep.

I said, That's an awfully thin line between good and bad.

She said, Actually, it's not that thin at all.

■　■　■

BEFORE LINCOLN AND KATYA headed back to Galveston the next morning, he and I went to get donuts. He said, Dada, which kind do you think I should get, one with sprinkles, or one with chocolate icing? I told him I thought he should get one of each. He said, That sounds good to me.

Standing below the drive-through window, where the parking

lot emptied into the street, a strategically savvy panhandler was hoping to collect change from donut lovers who would find it easier to give away their coins rather than put them in a purse. He had on a pair of Walkman headphones and a fat watch on his wrist. I drove by him and waved. Lincoln said, I think that man would get more money if he wasn't listening to his iPod and wearing a fancy watch.

Later that morning, we all sat in the conference room to iron out the narrative we would try to construct at the hearing that was ten days away. It had two strands. One was that there was no evidence at all that Quaker had committed the crime or that he should be on death row. The blood in his car had an innocent explanation, as did the life insurance. The fact that his gun had disappeared was curious, but hardly proof of murder. He did not have any blood or gunpowder residue on him when he was arrested. No one had seen him at the house. By all accounts, he adored his wife and kids. Mark Roberts had asked me how he could even have been convicted, and the answer to that question had two words: Jack Gatling. Quaker had a lawyer who was a burned-out case.

In theory, there is a presumption of innocence in the American legal system, innocent until proven guilty, but in practice, it is just the opposite. Juries trust the police and the prosecutors, especially when all the jurors are middle-class white folks, as they were at Quaker's trial. They think that if someone gets arrested and goes on trial, there must be good reasons to believe that he did it. Quaker's lawyer could have called the neighbors as witnesses and asked them whether they had ever heard Henry and Dorris fight. He could have asked them to describe how Henry interacted with Daniel and Charisse. He could have called Henry's coworkers. He could have called a scientific expert who would have explained that Henry would have had blood or gunpowder residue on himself and on his clothes and in his car if he had committed the crime. But Jack Gatling did none of those things.

Nor did he challenge the state's expert who single-handedly persuaded the jury to sentence Quaker to death. James Grigson is known as Dr. Death. He was expelled from the American Psychiatric Association as well as the Texas Society of Psychiatric Physicians, but that did not stop him from testifying in hundreds of trials. Grigson claimed to have examined somewhere between two hundred and four hundred capital-murder defendants—the number varied from case to case, because Grigson could not keep his answer straight from one trial to the next. But that did not stop juries from believing him. Sometimes he would not interview the defendants at all; other times he would visit with them for fifteen minutes or so in the county jail, asking them what they saw when they looked at ink blots. He would then sit on the witness stand for as much as five hours, telling jurors that the defendant before them would undoubtedly be dangerous in the future if not speedily put to death.

His flamboyant predictions were spectacularly wrong. By some estimates, he was wrong more than 95 percent of the time. But that too did not stop juries from believing him. Juries would even sentence people to death who had not committed any crime. In one famous case, Grigson testified that Randall Dale Adams would commit more violence if not executed. Adams had been convicted of murdering a state trooper outside of Dallas. Errol Morris made a documentary about the debacle of the trial. As it happened, Adams did not actually kill the officer; someone else did. Adams was released from prison after his innocence was established. He had not committed any crimes prior to his wrongful conviction, and he has not committed any since. But Grigson was nothing if not charming. His avuncular demeanor and white lab coat endeared him to juries. They did what he asked them to. He told them that Henry Quaker would be dangerous if they did not send him to the execution chamber, and the jury obliged.

When it was time for Quaker's trial lawyer to cross-examine the doctor, perhaps to ask him about the inconsistency in his numbers, or his expulsion from professional societies, or the many cases where his prognostications had proven so unsound, Jack Gatling stood up at the defense table and said, I have no questions for this witness. Gatling had been so convinced he would win an acquittal that he had not prepared even for the single witness that even he could have discredited.

Quaker had a spotless prison record. Part of our narrative would emphasize that Grigson had also been wrong in his case, and testimony from Nicole and other guards would help us there. But the problem we had was that this first theme in the narrative ultimately pivoted on the fact that Quaker's trial lawyer had been so inept, and even though he had been, it was too late for us to raise that claim. Some people think that law is about truth. It isn't, exactly. It is about timing. The time to prove that Henry Quaker did not kill anyone was years ago, at his trial, not now, a week and a half ahead of his scheduled execution.

But we also had a second strand to our narrative. We could

identify the murderer. His name was Ruben Cantu, and the proof that Cantu did it was the sworn words of Ezekiel Green.

Kassie said, It sure would be nice to know why Wyatt interviewed Cantu.

I said, I agree. Why don't you ask him?

Kassie said, Me? I've never met the guy. What makes you think he'll talk to me?

I said, Melissa Harmon told me that he got divorced six months ago, that he drinks every night at El Tiempo, and that he's a skirt hound. I'll pay for dinner if you get him to talk.

Gary said, You buying dinner for all of us?

I said, If she gets something useful from Wyatt, sure, why not.

Gary said, Hey Kass, be sure to wear something nice.

I said, That's my line, man.

Kassie said, Yeah, and it's just as clever, no matter who says it.

■　■　■

THE NEXT NIGHT, we were all sitting at El Tiempo, with a platter of mariscos a la parilla and beef fajitas. The amount this dinner was costing me was out of proportion to how hard Kassie had to work. She told Wyatt who she was and what she wanted to know, and he bought her a drink and told her. The neighbor who had seen the strange pickup truck parked in the street had remembered the last three numbers of the license plate. Wyatt did a computer search and came up with Cantu. He had arrested Cantu before for drug possession and decided he was worth talking to. Kassie asked why he hadn't arrested him, and Wyatt told her because he had no physical evidence, because Cantu had no motive, and because there was no evidence that Cantu even knew Dorris Quaker or her kids.

I asked Kassie whether she had asked him about the gun they found on the floor next to Dorris. She said, I'm not a moron.

And?

He looked right at me and said that he had no earthly idea what I was talking about.

Now I do not mean any disrespect by this, but police officers are some of the best liars in the world. Their philosophy seems to be, so far as I can tell, that they are the good guys fighting the forces of death and darkness, and that entitles them to break the rules when they think they need to and lie about it later when they deem it necessary. Wyatt would have sworn a lie on his dead mother's grave if he thought it would help him convict someone he was certain was guilty. If I knew anything, I knew that. But knowing means nothing. Proof is what matters, and I had no proof, and no prospects of getting any. Wyatt was not going to bare his soul, not to Kassie and certainly not to me, and every second I spent fantasizing that he would was another second I might as well have spent in prayer, for all the good it was going to do Quaker.

She said, He seems like a nice guy. He played football at LSU.

I said, Started dumb, finished dumb, too.

Jerome said, I know that one. It's Randy Newman, sort of.

When people start to get your references, it can be because you have become obvious and transparent. It can also be because they are learning.

That night at home I put on a Tony Bennett–Bill Evans CD and carried a snifter of cognac out to the patio. Bennett was singing My Foolish Heart and I was thinking about lines. Wyatt didn't care that he was lying and probably didn't even acknowledge that he was lying, because in the world where he lived, Quaker was guilty of a triple murder, and any facts that got in the way of that conclusion weren't facts at all. He used one set of concepts to make sense of the world. I use another. Why is that? I wondered. Why do some people care about ends and others care about means?

Last August we sat on the beach and watched the Perseid meteor shower. Hundreds of them fired across the sky. Lincoln kept saying, Look, there goes another one. I explained to him that we see them because the earth itself moves through the Perseid cloud. He said, It reminds me of dodgeball, Dada. It's lucky they don't hit us.

I looked up and found Orion. The hunter. I was just drunk enough to feel insightful, and the sky felt ominous. Our case hinged on a murderer we couldn't locate who had been identified by a murderer who was dead. Quaker was in big trouble. A part of me hoped he did it. A big part.

■ ■ ■

A WEEK BEFORE the hearing we got the results of the blood testing. The drops leading from Dorris's body to the spot where the kids were killed all belonged to Dorris. So unless she shot herself, went into the other room, murdered her two children, then walked back to the sofa, lay down, and died, she too had been murdered. It would be a lie to try to save Henry by pointing the finger at his wife.

Then again, there are only so many truths I can accommodate. Our finite lives have only so much capacity. You can't let every little truth exert an equal hold on you. It's called prioritization. My central truth was that Henry Quaker did not kill anyone. That truth and no other staked a claim on me. If I had to be less faithful to some other ancillary truths in order to demonstrate that fact, who could fault me? Who was even around to blame me? Dorris's dad was dead, and her mom was not exactly standing by Henry, but she wasn't blaming him, either. She seemed unsure what to think, and I didn't see her blowing any gaskets if I implied that Dorris killed herself. I don't think I could be an army general and send teenaged kids to their certain deaths. But Dorris was already dead. I didn't see the harm of killing her again.

Jerome thought it was a terrible idea, though, and he was right. At a trial, a lawyer can throw the whole platter of spaghetti at the wall and hope that a strand or two sticks. That's all it takes, one juror with one reasonable doubt. If Quaker's trial lawyer had not been comatose, he could have pursued that strategy. Point to Dorris, point to an intruder, point anywhere that was away from Henry. But it was too late for us to do that. At a trial, the defendant wins if it's a tie. At the stage we were at, a death-row inmate doesn't win unless it's a blowout. We had to prove that Quaker was innocent, and if we were going to succeed, we needed a single story. Our story was that Ruben

Cantu was the murderer. That was our story, and we were sticking to it.

What did we have? We would go over all the evidence of Gatling's incompetence. We would point out that the neighbor had seen a strange pickup in the driveway. We could suggest that the truck belonged to Cantu. (*Suggest* being a euphemism that meant we could not prove a damn thing.) We could prove that Wyatt had interviewed Ruben Cantu. And, for the coup de grace, we would pull out Green's declaration, stating that Cantu had murdered the Quaker family in a case of mistaken identity.

Gary said, Why do you even think the judge will let us put on any evidence of attorney incompetence?

Jerome added, And everything from Green is hearsay. She might not let in any of that evidence, either.

I said, It might be a short hearing.

■　■　■

*F*RUGALITY IS *the mother of all virtues.* Ben Jonson wrote that in 1598, in his play *Every Man in His Humour,* and the line is inscribed above the lintel of the twelve-story downtown office building where I sometimes work. My father is the cheapest—or, as he would say, the most frugal—man that I know. Once when we grilled hamburgers, someone in the group preferred his sandwich open-faced, so we were left at the end of dinner with the bottom half of a toasted bun. My father neatly wrapped it in wax paper and placed it in the freezer, next to a tub of Blue Bell Homemade Vanilla ice cream, where it remained for nearly eight months, until I gained the confidence that he would not miss it and dared to throw it away. For his seventy-fifth birthday, Katya took a picture of Lincoln and me, standing beneath the lintel, pointing up to it with our right hands, and holding half a burger bun in our lefts.

Some months later, I saw my brothers admiring the photograph I thought I had given to my dad. As it happened, they were in fact looking at a photograph of the building where I work, but it was not the picture taken by Katya of Lincoln and me. It was a picture that my grandfather took of the building in 1924, when he opened his law practice in the very same building where I now have an office on floor eleven. Visible on the third-floor window facing Main Street were the words *Harry Dow, Lawyer,* and the six-digit number of his office phone. No one in my family had any idea. The building is in decrepit disrepair and ought to be condemned, and we've been looking for new space for the past two years, but at that moment, I believed I belonged there.

My philosophy is: live well, love others, and hope that someone loves you. We live one life on this earth and then we return to dust. We have our bodies and our brains but nothing I would call a soul. I have no faith in higher powers, and I believe that there is no fate, but coincidence is nonetheless a real and curious thing. I keep the 1924 photograph hanging on my office wall, right next to a copy of the picture that Katya and I gave to my dad eighty years later. I touched my finger to it and decided to take a walk around the block. The day was cool and crisp.

It made me not want to smoke. I found myself at Treebeard's, where I had not aimed to be. I was not hungry. I walked inside, scanning the tables for Judge Truesdale. I bought a bowl of crabmeat gumbo and a bottle of Dixie beer and sat near the cash register, where I could see everyone who came through the line. I finished the first bottle and bought a second. I sat there for two hours wondering if she'd come in, wondering why I was wondering, until the manager locked the door, and the busboys ate leftover links of boudin sausage standing in the kitchen and began wiping down the tables and stacking the chairs.

■   ■   ■

SEVEN-EIGHTHS OF THE TIME, in the week leading up to the hearing, I was a monk. Lights out at eleven. Up at four. A forty-five-minute run, a half-hour swim, an orange, a banana, a bowl of Grape-Nuts and a pot of coffee, and at the office by seven. For twelve hours I'd cram like a medical student, memorizing every line on every document in every one of the dozen banker's boxes on the floor of my office. My plan was to be so busy that I had no time to appreciate how hopeless it was, but even hyperactivity cannot keep hopelessness at bay.

At precisely eight every night that week, like Swiss clockwork, my heart would start to race and my vision would blur and I would feel flushed even though my office window was open to the chilly air. I saw Quaker strapped down and his mother, Evelina, sitting in a wheelchair, watching through one-way glass, a canister of oxygen in her lap, plastic tubing running up her nose. I'd see flashing lights—my eye doctor calls them floaters—and I'd have to stand up and shake my head like a boxer beating the count to chase the image away. I'd walk two blocks to McElroy's and sit at the bar with a double Jack and a cigar. I'd call Lincoln to tell him a story before bed and then Katya would get on the phone and for the first time that day I quit pretending that I believed that everything was going to be all right. She and Lincoln would get on the phone together and tell me what they had done that day, about Schlitterbahn Waterpark or the Harry Potter movie or the long walk with Winona. In the mirror behind the bar I could see myself smile.

I'd drive home and make a sandwich. I thought, I wonder if Quaker is sleeping now? On our last visit, he told me that if he did not go to sleep, tomorrow would never come. I'd turn on the TV and drink just enough bourbon to keep Henry from visiting me again until the following day.

■   ▓   ■

THE HEARING WAS SCHEDULED to begin at eight thirty. We got there at eight. Judge Truesdale's clerk came up to me when we walked into the courtroom and said the judge wanted to see me for a moment in her chambers. Kassie cocked her head. Gary said, That's interesting.

She was wearing a short V-neck gray dress. Her legs were crossed and the bottom of the dress reached barely to the

201

middle of her thigh. She had on a necklace of what I think were diamonds that brushed the tops of her breasts. If she was aiming for sexy, she had definitely nailed it.

Here I should probably confess what is probably obvious, which is that I find women completely inscrutable. When I was a young lawyer in Washington, there was another lawyer at the firm, two or so years senior to me, who was my friend. Our offices were adjacent, so we would see each other every day and talk about ordinary things. A group of us would go out for a beer after work most evenings. Jane and I worked for the same boss. We'd talk about him and our work. Once, after I bought three dollars' worth of tunes from the jukebox, we discovered that we both played jazz piano just well enough to entertain ourselves and that neither one of us really understood Ornette Coleman. I said, You know the line in *Jerry Maguire* where Tom Cruise is at Renee Zellweger's house and she puts on a Miles Davis record and he says, What *is* this music? That's what I think about when I hear Ornette.

She said, People think it's a Miles Davis record, but it's actually Charlie Mingus. Anyway, don't tell anybody, but I feel that way, too.

Possibly she mistook my expression of surprise for something else. Our apartments were a block away from one another. As we were walking home from the bar, she grasped my hand in both of hers and said, What is going on between the two of us?

Later I would admire her forthrightness. But at the time, I was completely nonplussed. I didn't know what to say. I was impressed with her, not in love. I considered her just my friend and was pretty sure there was no good way to say that under the circumstances in a nonhurtful way. So I stood there, mute as an idiot. I had no earthly idea what I had done or said that would even make her question conceivable. How could she apparently be thinking something that had not even crossed within a thousand miles of my mind? Was she delusional, or was I? If you ponder that question for a moment or two, you realize that it has no good answer.

Subsequent evidence would indicate that I may have been the one with problems of perception. During my first year as a law professor, I was assigned the job of sitting in on a course taught by a practicing attorney. She was a trial lawyer, and the course was a practical one. We would visit briefly before each class. Afterward, while a group of students clustered around her to ask her more questions, I would wave and drive home. After the last class of the semester, we walked out to the parking lot together, and I told her how much I had enjoyed the class. It was not a line. I had enjoyed it. We got in our cars, but I had left my lights on, and the battery was dead. She offered to drive me home. When we pulled into my driveway, she asked if she could come inside and use the toilet. I was standing at the kitchen counter, sorting through the mail, when she walked out of the bathroom, wearing nothing.

At some point, when you think you see the world one way, but the rest of the world apparently sees it another, then, no matter how big your own ego happens to be, you need to acknowledge the numbers and concede that the world must be right, and that you are therefore wrong. That idea is what leapt into my brain as I sat there in Judge Truesdale's office. But Henry Quaker crowded her away. He was in a holding cell next to the courtroom, less than a hundred feet from where we were. He popped into a cartoon bubble, just like in *Annie Hall*, and whispered to me, Kiss her, man. Kiss her.

A prosecutor in a different case walked in with an order she wanted the judge to sign and leaned against the door frame. I told her hello. Judge Truesdale reached out her hand to take the order, but she kept her eyes on me. She said, I just wanted to tell you off the record that I've read everything you've written, or your associates have written, and I have real reservations about this case, but I am not sure there is anything I can do. From the corner of my eye I saw the prosecutor nod.

I said, Well, Judge, I think there is.

She said, We're off the record here. I'm Jocelyn.

I said, Jocelyn. We are going to ask you to withdraw the execution warrant.

Her right leg was crossed over her left. She said, Hmmm. She smoothed her skirt and brushed something invisible off. She stood up and said, Can you help me with my robe here?

■ ■ ■

CONTRARY TO OUR WORST FEARS, Judge Truesdale let us put on every piece of evidence we wanted. Maybe she really was bothered by the case. We called the insurance agent, who recalled that she had aggressively pushed a life insurance policy on Henry when he had been shopping for auto insurance.

The custodian of records for Daniel's pediatrician provided records that indicated that Daniel did in fact get frequent, spontaneous nosebleeds. Six guards said they believed Quaker was innocent and shouldn't be executed even if he wasn't. He was a model inmate, doing exactly what authorities asked him to. Detective Wyatt testified that he had interviewed Ruben Cantu because Cantu owned a truck with a license plate that could have meant it was the truck the neighbor saw in front of the Quakers' house. He said he never took Cantu seriously as a suspect, because, so far as he knew, Cantu did not know the Quaker family, but he also conceded that he had not looked into Cantu's alibi.

I did decide to ask him about having tested Dorris's hands for gunshot residue. He said it was routine. I said, Was it routine because you found a gun near her body? He said that there had not been a gun near the body. I said, So you thought she might have shot and killed herself and then disposed of the gun? The district attorney objected to that question and Judge Truesdale ruled in his favor and told Wyatt not to answer, but I was happy about that because I didn't want to trade this trivial battle for the bigger war. I just hadn't been able to help myself. I looked over at my team, making sure there wasn't anything I'd forgotten to cover. I noticed Henry. He was barely suppressing a glare. I had to turn away, like he was a flaming sun.

Henry was sitting between Kassie and me. Jerome and Gary were right behind us. The guards prefer that when death-row inmates are in court, no one is sitting between them. I asked the guard whether he wanted me to change places with Henry.

The guard folded his arms and shook his head. He said, Nah. Far as I'm concerned, he can stay right where he's at.

We had a tussle over Green's sworn statement. The hearsay rule prevents people from saying what other people supposedly said. The idea behind the hearsay rule is that the best evidence of whether someone said something is to ask her directly, rather than allowing someone else to give a secondhand report. But there are exceptions. Green's claim that he paid Cantu to kill Tricia Cummings was admissible under a doctrine known as a statement against interest. Because Green was saying something that incriminated himself, the judge could consider it. But his statement also reported what Cantu supposedly told him—that Cantu had mistakenly killed the Quaker family, and that he had left a gun there to make it look like suicide. That was hearsay, and the district attorney strenuously fought to keep it out of the record. In the end, the judge decided that she would think it over, and we did not really care what she decided, because either she believed Green or she didn't, and I was clinging to the hope that what she believed about what had happened would mean more to her than what she thought the rules of evidence allowed.

She asked us if we wanted to make a closing argument. We did. The prosecutor went first. He pointed at Quaker and said, Your Honor, a jury found this man guilty of murdering his wife and his two children. He turned and stared at Henry, and Henry looked back. He had a serenity to him, like he wasn't entirely there. I thought how Lauren Bacall reacted in *To Have and Have Not*, when the Vichy officer took her passport and slapped her in the face. Later, Humphrey Bogart told her that she hardly blinked an eye. I think it was because her hatred was tempered by understanding. At least that was how I interpreted Henry's stare.

The prosecutor reminded the judge that someone who has been convicted cannot overturn his sentence unless he can prove that every reasonable person would think he is innocent. We were nowhere close to satisfying that standard, the prosecutor said. There were any number of reasons—the insurance money, the blood in the car, the fact that Henry's marriage was in trouble—to believe that he might have done it. If there was any reason to believe he might have done it, the judge's hands were tied.

Everything the prosecutor said was correct. The law might not have been on our side, but principle was. When it was my turn, I reminded the judge that the only reason Quaker had ever been convicted was that his lawyer was so bad. I stuck to our story: that the evidence of guilt was massively underwhelming, and that there was good reason to think that Cantu had committed the murders.

Judge Truesdale said, I sure would like to hear from Mr. Cantu. Where is he?

I said, I'd like to know that, too, Judge.

We'd gotten Cantu's DNA off the orange juice carton, but he was not in any police databases. He could have been dead, back in Mexico, or living next door.

She banged her gavel, and we were done. We stood as she walked out. As we were packing up our files, one of the guards who would escort Henry back to death row came over and said to me, Good luck, sir.

■　■　■

WE'D GOTTEN A SHORT LETTER from Walter Buckley. He was scheduled to be executed in two days. He had sent it two weeks earlier but it took awhile to reach us because he had misspelled literally every word in my address. He was not my client. He was being represented (using that term in its loosest possible sense) by Karl Christianson, a notoriously inept lawyer. Under a Supreme Court case called *Atkins v. Virginia*, the states are not permitted to execute people who are mentally retarded. It was difficult to figure out exactly what Buckley was talking about, but it seemed he was writing to say that his lawyer had never raised an Atkins claim. If true, this was an unimaginable dereliction. One criterion of mental retardation is an IQ of 70 or below. According to our database, Buckley had an IQ of 54. Based on his letter, I would have thought it was even lower.

As usual, Jerome felt like we needed to do something. I felt like we couldn't. Quaker's execution was a week away. And even though we had already written everything that I expected we would need to write, you never know. Things always come up. We didn't know how Judge Truesdale was going to rule, and if she ruled tomorrow, I'd want to turn our attention immediately to appealing if we lost, or to holding on to our victory, if we won. I also wanted to meet with the members of the Board of Pardons and Paroles, who had the power to recommend that Quaker be released from prison, or at least moved off of death row, and to talk to the governor and the warden. We couldn't be jumping into a case about which we knew almost nothing less than forty-eight hours before an execution. I said so.

Presaged by the envelope, virtually every word in Buckley's

letter to us was also misspelled. He used quotation marks apparently at random and no punctuation except commas, again seemingly randomly placed. Maybe he was retarded. Maybe, too, Christianson had raised an Atkins claim, and Buckley didn't realize it. Who knew?

Jerome said, Is it okay for me at least to call Christianson and see if he raised the claim and get whatever records he has?

You don't have to be hard-hearted to do this work, but you have to develop some defenses. We can't save everyone. We can't even try to save everyone.

I said, Sure. Go ahead.

▪ ▪ ▪

My brother Steven was in town for the day on business, and he had brought with him his daughter Hannah, who is Lincoln's age, so the two cousins could play. I got home an hour before they would head to the airport. The kids wanted to have a relay race against the dads. The rules were numerous, if not complicated. In good nature, I repeatedly violated one rule. I was just clowning around, but seven-year-olds don't always laugh at the same things I do. Lincoln began to get angry and raise his voice. He told me not to cheat. I told him not to scream at me and promptly cheated again. He raised his voice again. I told him that if he did it one more time the game was over, and I cheated again. His entire body tensed up and he shouted at me, Stop cheating, Dada.

I said, That's it. Game's over, amigo. Tell Hannah and Uncle Steven good night and go get ready for bed.

Dada, you're being too hard on me.

I pointed toward his room. He stormed up the stairs. I walked into the kitchen and poured myself a drink. Steven followed me in while Hannah stood by the front door. I asked whether Hannah would be disappointed if they left without finishing the game. He said, She will be, but don't worry about that.

Steven and his wife have three children. Hannah is the youngest. I asked whether he thought I had been too tough. Steven said, He seemed to me like he was trying to control himself. You got him pretty mad.

I said, He needs to learn to do what I say, no matter how mad he is.

Steven said, I agree.

I said, I'll go upstairs and get him. We'll be right down.

After we finished the game, and lost, of course, with me playing strictly by the rules, and after Lincoln had brushed his teeth and we had read a book and told a story and sung a song, I said, Amigo, I'm sorry I cheated and made you mad, but when Mama or I or Nana or one of your teachers tells you what to do, you have to do it, even if you don't want to, and even if it makes you really mad. Can you try to do that?

He said, I'll try, Dada. But it's hard sometimes. I told him I knew, but I wanted him to try hard. He said, Okay, I will. Will you sleep with me for five minutes?

I'm no expert on the Holocaust, but I do know that one group of scholars blames the tragedy on an essential feature of the German personality. Katya and I have discussed this, of course. When we were in Germany visiting her relatives, she pointed out to me all the ways that Germans defer to authorities that Americans do not even notice. Once, riding the train from Manhattan to New Haven, she commented on how the riders were oblivious to the conductors as they walked through the cars asking for tickets. On German trains, the riders treat conductors like they are lords. It's the uniform.

Which is worse, too much deference, or not enough? How do you insist to a child that he do what others say, without raising him to be an adult who says he had to do what he did because someone told him to?

■　■　■

TEN HOURS BEFORE Buckley's execution, at eight o'clock on Thursday morning, Jerome walked into my office with a sheaf of papers and reported that Buckley had dropped out of school in the seventh grade, that he had taken three IQ tests and scored between 53 and 59 on all of them, that he had never been able to live by himself, that three doctors, including one employed by the state, had deemed him mentally retarded, and that, in spite of all that, his lawyer, Attorney Christianson, had decided not to raise a claim that Buckley's retardation made him immune from execution. I asked Jerome why not. He said, Christianson told me that when he went to visit Buckley, Buckley just didn't seem that slow.

Kassie and Gary were doing research to determine whether

there was some way that Judge Truesdale could call off Quaker's execution in a way that would not allow the state to appeal to a higher court. I called them into my office, and the four of us debated. It wasn't much of a debate. I was the only one suggesting that we were too busy to do anything, and that there wasn't enough time besides, but it's hard to be passionate in advancing the proposition that we should stand idly by and allow the state to execute someone who the Constitution says can't be executed. They overruled me again.

The harder question was what to do. I wrote three lines on the whiteboard in my office: the Supreme Court, the federal court of appeals, state court. The problem with the first option was that the last time the Supreme Court ruled in favor of someone who had used the legal device we would be forced to use was in the 1930s. We'd spend a lot of time writing with virtually no prospect of victory. I scratched through it. The problem with the court of appeals was even larger. Many of the judges on that court are an embarrassment, and I was still thinking about the way they had gone home the night of O'Neill's scheduled execution. In addition, federal law mandates that, with few exceptions, inmates present their legal claims to state court before proceeding to federal court. I knew we couldn't satisfy any of the exceptions in Buckley's case, and I couldn't even think of a decent argument for saying that we could. State court is what we were left with.

But even getting in to state court would be a challenge. We had to present significant evidence that Buckley was in fact retarded, and we had to explain why it took us so long to locate the evidence. Proving he was retarded was not going to be the problem. Explaining why we were coming forward with the proof only hours before the execution was. The truthful answer is that the court-appointed lawyer who had represented Buckley for the past two years had not done his job, but that is not a winning answer. Under federal law, Buckley did not have a constitutional right to have any lawyer at all. Therefore, even if Buckley's lawyer was comatose, he still got more than he was entitled to. I told Gary, Kassie, and Jerome to divide up writing the part of the petition that would lay out the evidence of Buckley's retardation, and I would try to come up with some explanation for why we should be allowed to raise the claim at this, the eleventh hour.

The federal courts accept emergency pleadings by e-mail. The state court does not. We have an office in Austin, where the court is located. We let them know that we would be sending them the Buckley petition later that afternoon. They would make a dozen copies and run them across town to the court. At two that afternoon I finished what I was working on and asked Jerome to send me what they had. I made some revisions, combined our two parts into a single document, and sent it back to Jerome, so he and the others could put it in the proper format for filing. Actually, what I should say is that I tried to send it. It wouldn't go through. Our whole computer network had crashed.

Initially I was calm. I called Austin and told them to call the court and let them know we might be a few minutes late. It was nearly four. Austin called back. The clerk of the court had said that they close at five on the dot. I didn't have time for this. Gary was trying to get our computer system running. I screamed at Kassie to deal with the clerk. She called the court of appeals again and insisted that the clerk tell his superiors that we were planning to file something for Walter Buckley, who was scheduled to be executed in two hours, that we had finished writing it, and that we were experiencing catastrophic computer failure, which was delaying our delivery of the petition. He called her back and said that the presiding judge of the court said that the court closes at five o'clock.

At four thirty Gary got everything restored. It was going to be close. We e-mailed the document to Austin. Including exhibits, it was 107 pages long. They printed it and made the required copies. They called the court to let them know they were on the way. The clerk answered. It was not quite ten past five. He said, The court closed at five. The paralegals drove over anyway. The door was locked, and no one came to open it when they banged.

We had a problem. It was almost five thirty, and the papers that we had been working on for the Supreme Court were based on the assumption that we had lost in state court, not on the assumption that we had never managed to get anything filed in that court. We couldn't file an appeal from the state court's decision, because there was no state court decision. I won't bore you with the details of why this is a complicated problem, but it is. So I quickly wrote something up, asking the Supreme Court to issue a stay of execution, promising the justices that we would get something filed in the state court the following day. I knew as we were e-mailing it to the Court at minutes before six that it had all kinds of technical legal problems, but I hoped they would not matter, that what the justices would focus on was the fact that Buckley had an IQ score somewhere in the mid-50s. But hope is an impotent indulgence. One day soon, I swear, I am going to give up on it completely. The justices unanimously turned us down.

By the time I called Buckley to tell him the news, at a few minutes after six, they had already strapped him to the gurney. I did not get to tell him that our pleas had been turned away because the judges do not really care about principles or justice. I did not get to tell him that we had tried, and that I was sorry. I did not have to tell him that if our office had state-of-the-art computers, he would have lived to see another day.

Gary came into my office. His eyes were swollen. He said, This is my fault. I should have replaced that server six months ago.

I said, Pal, there is a long list of people whose fault it is, including nine in Austin and nine more in Washington, and your name is not on it.

I called Katya with the news. I asked her to put Lincoln to bed without me and told him a story over the phone. I gathered up the team and we walked next door to Cafe Adobe. We went through two pitchers of margaritas without exchanging barely a word. At nine I stood up, told them they were the best lawyers I knew, and that I'd see them in the morning.

■   ■   ■

ON THE SIDE of the freeway, a woman standing next to a pickup truck with a blown-out front tire was frantically waving her arms. I stopped. She had no cell phone and wanted to use mine to call a tow truck. I didn't think I would feel comfortable driving away before the wrecker got there, so it seemed just as easy to change the tire. I pulled the truck as close to the shoulder as I could, turned on the flashers, and asked her to stand a ways up the road to wave people away from the shoulder. Twenty minutes later she was good to go. She had a folded-over stack of bills in her hand that was two inches thick. She said, Please, take this. Buy yourself dinner. I told her there was not a chance. She said, Please. I am going to feel terrible if you don't.

I said, Ma'am, I promise you that I will feel worse if I do. She said thank you a half dozen times. Disproportionate gratitude, I believe, is always sincere.

I waited for her to drive off, then pulled onto the freeway behind her. At home I checked on Lincoln and told Katya the story. She became angry. She wanted me to file an official grievance with the judicial conduct commission. She wanted us to hold a press conference. I wanted to share her sense of outrage, but I couldn't. I felt peaceful.

The definition of lucky in life is a wife and son and dog like mine to come home to, and the good fortune to have not the slightest inclination or need to take a couple of hundred bucks a stranger is offering as compensation for doing a tiny act of kindness that any decent human being would do.

■   ■   ■

KATYA AND I both have five names on our lists. They are the celebrities we have given each other permission to sleep with, should the occasion ever present itself. All married couples have these lists, right?

Last winter a cab driver in Utah told me that her best friend and the friend's husband had the same arrangement. Angelina Jolie was on his list. The week before, during the Sundance Film Festival, Jolie was standing in front of him at the Starbucks in Park City. He was a ski instructor in the winter and a raft guide in the summer. He probably made less than $25,000 a year. He told her that the latte was on him. I am clearly not the only delusional man in America.

Judge Truesdale called my cell phone. She invited me to coffee on Tuesday afternoon, the day before the execution. I was pretty sure Katya was wrong about her and I was right. Once we were watching a movie where a man called his wife to say he was working late. He went to a hotel with a client. When he got home, his wife, son, and daughter were eating dinner in the kitchen. He kissed his wife and then his children. Katya said, I could forgive you if you were to cheat on me, but if you kiss me when you get home afterward I'll kill you. It was an empty gesture. There are two kinds of men: those who can cheat, and the ones who can't. I'm not saying that either is better than the other. I'm just saying that Katya knew which group I was in.

When Ezekiel Green called me from death row on a cell phone he was not supposed to have, I didn't want to know the terms of his barter. Now I did. Perhaps it is possible to be unfaithful without being disloyal.

■   ■   ■

In 1924, CLARENCE DARROW saved Nathan Leopold and Richard Loeb from the gallows. The two young men had kidnapped and murdered a young boy named Bobby Franks, just to see if they could. Leopold and Loeb might not have been geniuses, but they were both supremely bright. Darrow made the astonishing decision to eschew a jury. His clients pleaded guilty, and Darrow threw their fate at the feet of the judge:

> Your Honor, it may be hardly fair to the court. I am aware that I have helped to place a serious burden upon your shoulders....I have always meant to be your friend. But this was not an act of friendship. I know perfectly well that where responsibility is divided by twelve, it is easy to say: "Away with him." But, Your Honor, if these boys hang, you must do it. There can be no division of responsibility here. You can never explain that the rest overpowered you. It must be by your deliberate, cool, premeditated act, without a chance to shift responsibility.

What Darrow understood is that our system of capital punishment survives because it is built on an evasion. It permits everyone to avoid responsibility. A juror is one of twelve, and therefore the decision is not hers. A judge who imposes a jury's sentence is implementing someone else's will, and therefore the decision is not his. A judge on the court of appeals is one of three, or one of nine, and professes to be constrained by the decision of the finder of fact, and therefore it is someone else's call. Federal judges say it is the state court's decision. The Supreme Court justices simply say nothing, content to permit the machinery of death to grind on with their tacit acquiescence.

Darrow didn't let them hide. He demanded that people who uphold the law take responsibility for their actions, especially when those actions are momentous. I think he was right. Jurors and judges who send someone to the gallows should be required to witness their deed and observe the execution. Every court of appeals judge who upholds a death sentence should have to visit death row and deliver the news personally. Supreme Court justices who refuse to grant a death-row inmate a stay of execution should have to deliver the news face-to-face to the inmate as he waits in the holding cell eight steps down the dank hall from the execution chamber, instead of having one of their law clerks call the inmate's lawyer. If we are going to execute people in our society because we believe that it is an appropriate punishment for people who callously and irresponsibly take another's life, then the people with the power not to execute ought to take responsibility themselves for imposing the punishment, or at least not negating it. It's easier to kill somebody if it's someone else's decision, and if somebody else does the killing. Our death-penalty regime depends for its functionality on moral cowardice.

In Texas, the most gutless of all is the governor. If he wanted authority to decide for himself whether a convicted murderer should be spared, the legislature would give it to him in a heartbeat, but he doesn't. He hides behind the jury, and behind the courts, and most of all, behind the Texas Board of Pardons and Paroles. The Board consists of seven feckless people who gave him a lot of money. The governor appoints them to six-year terms, and they do what they think he wants them to. If the Board rec-

219

ommends that an inmate be spared, the governor can go along with that recommendation or not, but if the Board votes against the inmate, then the governor's hands are tied. Governors, like George W. Bush and Ann Richards, want the Board to turn the inmate down, and, through back channels, they let their cronies know that. Later, they stand outside the governor's mansion and shrug their shoulders and say that the inmate received a fair trial, that it was reviewed by the courts, that his appeal for clemency was turned down by the Board, and that there is nothing they can do. Then they head off to dinner at the Four Seasons and talk about bearing the weight of permitting someone to die.

Is there any phrase in the English lexicon more immoral than *There was nothing I could do*?

But some people are changed by responsibility. Paul Brownwell, a cattle rancher in Giddings, was one of them. He called me at my office at seven o'clock on Monday night. He said, I wanted you to know before we tell the press that the Board just voted against recommending commutation in Mr. Quaker's case. The vote was four to three. I'm just sick about it. It was the best clemency petition I've ever read. I'm sorry to be telling you this.

I thanked him for the call. I walked into the conference room where the others were eating a pizza and told them the news. We have among us fifty years of death-penalty experience, but everyone was stunned. In the extraordinary case—with an inmate who is mentally retarded, for example—we expect the Board to recommend relief. In the typical case, we expect the Board to deny relief, usually by a vote of seven to nothing. We had little experience with a vote of four to three. I had thought the clemency petition was a waste of time. It turns out that the real waste of time was not spending another hour on it to try to pick up one more vote. I'm not a cheerleader, but their faces were breaking my heart. I said, It's not even close to over. We've got lots of arrows left in the quiver.

What I didn't say was that I had a bad feeling we had already used the one with the sharpest point. I didn't need to. They didn't believe a word I was saying.

■   ■   ■

Tuesday afternoon Judge Truesdale called and asked whether we could meet for a drink at the Magnolia instead of coffee at Diedrich. She was sitting at a table in the back when I got there. The waiter came over and I asked him for club soda with lime. She said, I'll have another. Bring him one, too.

When I'm in a bar or restaurant and I run into a judge presiding over one of my cases, I become a stick figure. I want to say what I think, but I feel like I can't, and it is a short step from there to feeling like I am someone else, someone I recognize but do not really know, the way most people know their neighbors. I used to think it was because of ethical restrictions on what lawyers are supposed to say to judges about cases pending in their courtrooms, but that's not really it. It is because they are not mortal. They hold the power to spare my client. For a short moment in a tiny space, they are God. I want to know what they are thinking, so that if they are thinking wrong, I can try to nudge them. If Moses can rebuke Yahweh, I can implore a judge. I want them to see the human reasons my client deserves to live, not the legal ones. I want them to be moral agents, not judges. But Moses turned away from the burning bush. I know exactly what I will say, and I also know I won't.

When Katya was practicing law, she negotiated settlements with insurance companies. She would quibble over every last dime. When someone knocks on our door asking if we want him to power-wash the exterior of our house, she pays him whatever he asks. It is easier to negotiate on someone else's behalf. But sometimes it can be hard to separate your own interests from your client's.

I thought to myself, I will not be begging for my own life. I will be pleading for someone else who ought to live. No one has done that for him. Someone needs to. It is the very least he deserves.

Our drinks came. She raised her glass. I picked up my glass of soda to clink against hers. She nodded to the martini the waiter had also set in front of me and said, Use that one.

She said, What do you want to talk about? I told her I was uncomfortable discussing the case. I had no idea why I was there if I was not going to talk about the case, but there I was. I'd stew over that contradiction later. There were two olives in her drink. She used her thumb and index finger to lift one out. She ate it, then put both fingers in her mouth together to lick off the brine. Under the table her right leg was crossed over her left. She leaned forward. I felt her toes against my shin. She said, I walked here from my office. When I drink too much, I stay the night. I've already checked in. Bring your drink and come upstairs with me.

She was wearing a black silk blouse open at the neck and a string of pearls. She tucked a strand of loose hair behind her ear. I wondered whether I would tell Katya. It's one thing to sleep with someone because you want to. It's a different thing to sleep with someone because you want them to do something. I once told Katya that I couldn't sleep with any of the famous people on my list because if I did I wouldn't know myself anymore, and if I didn't know myself, I'd have to kill myself. I can't live with a stranger. She had said, No one knows himself as well as he thinks he does, including you. People surprise themselves all the time.

In college I memorized chunks of Saint Augustine's Confessions. *Future things then are not yet: and if they be not yet, they are not. And if they are not, they cannot be seen.* If you could alter history with a minor transgression, wouldn't you do it? Wouldn't it be immoral not to?

She signaled the waiter and showed him her room key. She said, Put this on my bill. She stood up and drank down the rest of her martini. She leaned over and her lips were nearly touching my ear. I smelled the gin on her breath. I felt heat coming off her face. I felt her breasts pressing against my shoulder. She said, I think you'll find it worthwhile. I felt a drop of sweat in my armpit. She whispered, Come on.

I saw Quaker in his cell, sitting on his metal cot, reading. Everything was dark, except for the book, illuminated by the 25-watt bulb of a small gooseneck lamp. I saw the crime scene photographs: Dorris, Daniel, and Charisse, their skin hued yellow, their blood almost black. I saw Lincoln sleeping. I heard Quaker say, In case you're wondering, I didn't kill my family.

I said, Judge, I can't do this.

■ ■ ■

A VAN BACKED UP to a loading dock at the Polunsky Unit at
two o'clock. Half an hour before, guards had led a shackled
Quaker to the shower and given him fresh clothes. He felt nothing, neither courage nor fear, neither bitterness nor forgive-
ness, neither hatred nor love. He could not recall whether he
had requested a final meal. He had written his mother a letter
and had asked the warden to mail it once it was over. He told
her about it when he talked to her on the phone that morning and told her good-bye. She would not be watching him die.
He stood under the hottest water he could stand while three
guards watched him, their hands resting on holstered cans of
Mace they knew they would never need to use. He dressed and
walked into the back of the Chevy van. One of the guards said,
Inmate Quaker, I hope I see you tomorrow. Quaker nodded,
his eyes soft. The other two guards got in the van. The one who
had spoken wiped away a tear.

■ ■ ■

I TALKED TO HENRY just after he arrived at the Walls Unit at
four and told him about the vote of the Board. I reminded him
that we still had a petition pending in the Supreme Court, but
that we all expected it to be denied. I told him that our indica-
tions were that Judge Truesdale was going to deny our request
for a stay. I didn't tell him why I was sure of that. He hadn't said
a word. I knew he was still on the line because I could hear

electric doors clanging shut in the background. He said, You'll be here watching tonight, right?

At five o'clock, Judge Truesdale called. She said, You're not Joan of fucking Arc, you know. I was not sure how to respond to that. She said, I just signed an order withdrawing the date.

I said, Thank you, Judge. She hung up without another word.

The others were in Jerome's office, discussing whether there was a way to create a legal claim out of the fact that Judge Truesdale had not issued a ruling. I told them she had called. I asked Kassie to call the district attorney's office to confirm. She said, To confirm? You don't believe her?

I said, Just call.

Ten minutes later they were standing in my office. Kassie had talked to Shirley in the DA's office. Shirley believed that Judge Truesdale did not have any legal authority to withdraw the execution date. Under state law, unless a legal action challenging a death sentence is pending in state court, the trial judge cannot issue a stay of execution. The DA's office interpreted *legal action* narrowly, and it was true that we had not yet filed a traditional challenge to Quaker's conviction. Our theory was that we were entitled to gather the evidence to support our claim that he was innocent, and then file a claim based on his actual innocence after we had gathered the evidence. We believed that so long as we were using the judicial process to gather that evidence, which we were, the trial judge could intervene and halt the execution. Kassie explained that to Shirley. Shirley was unimpressed. Shirley told Kassie that the district attorney's office was going to appeal.

Here's why I could never be a prosecutor: because I could never be *driven* to kill someone. I understand death-penalty supporters. I used to be one. I can relate to the retributive impulse. I know people I want to kill. I've tried my hardest to save all my clients, but some executions don't make me cry. There is very little that fire-and-brimstone Bible thumpers and I agree on when it comes to issues of crime and punishment. I believe the world would be better off without religion. But we do have one thing in common: I believe in evil. There are people who commit acts of cruelty so monstrous you have to barricade your senses from contemplating them because if you don't their images will ruin every pleasure you know. When you are petting your dog, hugging your son, kissing your wife, they will slither in between you and the object of your affection and make you ashamed to be human. That's why I shower when I get home from the prison and wash my clothes in a load of their own. I have friends who quit doing this work because they couldn't keep the images from burrowing deep down into their consciousness and stealing all their joy. I doubt the evil men I know were born that way, but maybe some were. Nobody really knows. But I'll also tell you this: Even the worst people I've ever known are sympathetic strapped to a gurney. They're no longer cruel or evil. Some are repentant, some aren't. What they all are, at that moment, are helpless, deeply broken men.

I have a recurring dream: Someone has killed everyone I love. He's tied to a chair, his arms cuffed behind him, his legs bound. There's a blue bandana tied around his throat and he can barely breathe. Both he and I are bloody and bruised. I whip him with a gun. His head sags. Blood is pouring from his mouth and nose. I reach my right arm out and press the barrel to his left temple. He is not defiant. He is not contrite. And always, moments before I wake, I try to imagine how this is going to feel.

In the Hebrew Bible, the government does not carry out executions. The death penalty is inflicted by the *goel*, the avengers, family members of the victim. In Islamic law, the family can spare from death the criminal who caused them harm. I think that if we are going to have the death penalty, the family members should carry out the executions. Some of them would do it. Maybe I would, too.

But not in the dream. In the dream I drop the gun. It clatters to the floor, and I walk away. It's not a betrayal not to feel a need to kill.

At five thirty the clerk from the Supreme Court called to tell me that our petition had been turned down. He asked whether we were going to be filing anything else. This is a boilerplate question that he always asks, and the answer is always no. He wants to go home. The law clerks want to go home. The justices want to be able to concentrate on their poker games. A judge on the court of appeals once wrote an article saying it was hard on him to be at dinner parties on the night of an execution because the possibility that a last-minute appeal might be filed made it hard for him to enjoy himself. When I told the clerk that I was not yet sure I could feel him stiffen. He thought I was being flip. He had not heard that the judge had withdrawn the date and that the state was appealing. I said, Sorry for making y'all stay late tonight.

I called Henry again. It was about the time they'd move him

from the holding cell to the execution chamber. The guard who answered the phone was unusually polite. He used the word *sir* three times in our three-second conversation. Hello, sir. Yes sir, he is right here. One moment, sir. I told Henry that Judge Truesdale had withdrawn the date. He did not say anything, but he must have reacted. I heard the guard saying, What is it? Henry told me to hold on, and I heard him tell the guards. I heard one of them shout, All right!

I told him that the DA was appealing and we were a long way from out of the woods. He said, I don't even count the chickens once they've hatched. I wait till they're supper.

That's what he said, but in his voice I thought I could hear relief.

■ ■ ■

AT JUST PAST SIX, we got a copy of the district attorney's appeal. The argument was brief. They wrote that because no appeal was pending in Judge Truesdale's court, she did not have any authority to withdraw the execution date, and they requested that the court of appeals order her to reinstate it. We were in the conference room. I zinged my Super Ball off the thick glass door. I said, I think they blew it. Everyone looked at me. I said, They asked the court of appeals to order Judge Truesdale to reset the date. I don't think they can do that. Setting an execution date is a discretionary act, and courts of appeals cannot order lower-court judges to do something if that something is discretionary. I paused to see whether anyone disagreed. No one did. I said, I guess we should file a response, just in case.

Gary started to crank it out. All he planned to write was that the court of appeals had no authority to order Judge Truesdale to do what the DA had requested. But the court of appeals beat us to it. At seven we got their opinion. Gary said, This is unbelievable. They gave them a friggin' road map.

It was true. But now here is what you have to understand to appreciate exactly what we were feeling: When the court of appeals rules against us, as they do pretty much all the time, they ordinarily just tell us that we lose, and that's it. You can write a sophisticated appeal that is three hundred pages long, and the court of appeals will say, We've considered your argument, and we reject it. They do not tell you why; they do not reveal their thinking; they do not tell you which features of your argument they don't accept. They just say: You lose. But not this time. The court of appeals wrote:

Under state law, a court of appeals may not compel a lower court to perform a discretionary act. However, when a lower court's act is ultra vires, the court of appeals has authority to overrule that act and restore the status quo ante. Because we have not been asked to do so, we express no opinion on the desirability of such correction in the current proceeding.

Ultra vires is legalese for *beyond its authority*. That phrase made my heart race. The court of appeals was agreeing with the DA.

One Saturday night when I was fourteen and my brother Steven was ten, he was cooking himself a hamburger for dinner. I flipped it from the skillet onto the floor. The dog ate it in a flash. Steven waited up for my parents to get home and told them what I had done. My dad asked him how he thought I should be punished. Steven proposed that I be forced to go a week without dinner. My dad said, That seems a little severe. What if he had to cook you a new hamburger tonight and another one tomorrow? Steven said that sounded like a good idea to him, and so that's what happened.

It is a grievous insult to my honorable and deeply principled father to have been reminded of that childhood episode by the Texas court, but there it was. The court of appeals told the DA that they could not correct the problem the way the district attorney had asked them to, then added that the district attorney had not asked them to do the one thing they *did* have the power to do. I could see my brother Steven nodding at my dad's advice. And despite what some others may tell you, the district attorneys are not imbeciles. At eight o'clock they sent us a copy of their newest filing, which was identical to the previous one, save for the last page, on which they asked the court of appeals to declare that the decision withdrawing the execution date was void and of no effect, and that the warden was therefore still under an order to carry out the execution before midnight. At eight fifteen the court of appeals issued an order saying that Judge Truesdale's attempt to nullify the execution date was null and void.

■   ■   ■

EVERY CASE HAS its own unique moment of panic where the last best hope has just evanesced and the only honest corner of your rational brain tries to convince the rest of your emotional and effectively delusional self that you can keep pulling the trigger for as long as you want but the target has left the room, but of course if you were rational you would have stopped doing this work long ago when you realized that nearly all your clients end up dead, so you horde a hundred tricks, a thousand, for convincing yourself that what appears to be reason is actually surrender, and surrender is never reasonable, or at least never honorable, and so you start firing wildly like Jodie Foster in *Silence of the Lambs* where she can't see an inch in front of her face but is going to go down shooting, and just because it's a movie doesn't mean it couldn't really happen that way, and so you are convinced that the fact that she killed the bad guy means that you will, too. Justice will prevail.

Jerome said, We need to file an original writ.

Ah Jerome, my very own Jodie Foster.

An original writ is an appeal filed directly in the U.S. Supreme Court. Most pleadings that are filed in the Supreme Court are appeals from a lower appellate court's ruling. We had not filed anything in any lower court of appeals. We had placed all our eggs in one basket, the highly remote possibility that Judge Truesdale would do the right thing, and our million-to-one shot had paid off. If it had failed, we would have filed something. Once it succeeded, we relaxed. How many ways could we have been wrong? We didn't expect to succeed. When we did, we didn't expect the DA to appeal. When they did, we didn't expect the court of appeals to intervene. When they did, we didn't expect them to do the DA's work for them. I had explanations for all these decisions, but as I tell my students at the law school, if you're explaining, you're losing. The bottom line is that there was nothing we could appeal to the Supreme Court, and it was too late to file anything in the lower courts. So in a way, Jerome was right. This is known as the mathematics of small numbers. When there is only one option, that option is the right answer.

I did not need to remind him that we were coming up on the hundred-year anniversary of the last time the Supreme Court ruled in favor of a death-row inmate on an original writ, because he already knew. Our lone option was a puny, shriveled, impotent protest.

I said, Go ahead. Tell the Court it's coming. I'll call the governor and tell them we're filing a reprieve request. Then I'm going to the prison. Call me every ten minutes.

In several moments of realistic lucidity, anticipating this southern turn, I had drafted a letter to the governor, laying out the argument that Quaker was innocent, and would have been found innocent if his lawyer had not been inept. I asked Kassie and Gary to tinker with it and send it by e-mail. Gary was in Kassie's office, his hand resting on her shoulder. They looked lovely together, and I thought I was going to cry. How could I know so little about the lives of these people with whom I spent so much time? To how much of the world was I utterly oblivious?

■   ■   ■

THE PRISON WAS two hours away. I did not have two hours. I had maybe an hour and a half. I had called and told the warden I was coming. I asked them not to move Quaker out of the holding cell until ten. That would still give them two hours to carry out their protocol, more than enough time. They told me they would wait until exactly ten, not a minute later.

During the daytime, the drive from Houston to Huntsville is beautiful. The piney forest presses against the interstate from both the east and the west. At night, it's inky black. Once I got north of Conroe, the road was empty and dark. Kassie called every ten minutes, just as I had requested. Every call went like this: I'd answer by saying, Any news? She'd say, No, nothing yet. I'd say, Thanks for the update. Talk to you in ten.

I had no interest in being alone with my absence of ideas. I called Katya. I told Lincoln good night. I turned on a country music station. Katya once suspected that her iPod has a brain, because the random shuffles produce perfect juxtapositions. It's just math, I said, not divine intervention. I wish she had been there with me. Gordon Lightfoot was singing about books you won't read because the endings are too sad. It was too obvious to be ominous. I changed to a Motown station. There was Gladys Knight, right on cue to challenge my rationality, singing a song about saying good-bye. Proximity to death is religion's most successful proselytizer.

When I was taking flying lessons, before my first solo flight, Quan—the instructor—and I headed out over the Katy Prairie. It was a perfect day, not a cloud in sight, not a whisper on the radar. I turned south and flew us toward the Gulf of Mexico. But summer weather on the Gulf Coast can be confounding, and a dense fog blew in fast. The typically calm Quan took the controls and said, a little too loudly, I'm flying the plane. You couldn't see a thing. He was flying by the instruments, but they don't help you see the runway. The wind was ferocious. I did not know enough to be scared, but when Quan finally flew us into visibility, he opened his window, lit a cigarette, and shook one out of the pack at me. I suddenly started shaking so hard that the cigarette fell from my mouth. It rolled under the seat. Quan said, Dive. I looked at him. He said, You're flying now. Dive the plane. I did. The cigarette appeared. Quan reached over and picked it up, then he stuck it back in my mouth.

Lessons in life are context specific. Contexts are never the same. If there are no lessons you can use, does that mean there are actually no lessons? Driving to the prison, I struck a match to light a cigar and somehow dropped it. I couldn't very well make a car dive. I reached down to put out the flame before my car caught fire, and when I did my front right tire briefly ran onto the shoulder. At nearly a hundred miles an hour, it made quite a racket. I yanked the car back into my lane. I almost laughed out loud, imagining killing myself on my way to an execution, imagining what the hell else could go wrong. That's when the flashing lights appeared behind me.

■　■　■

I PULLED ONTO THE RIGHT-HAND SHOULDER and left the engine running. I was looking out my sideview mirror, hoping to get a measure of his attitude from his gait. The trooper managed to approach my car from the passenger side, completely out of my sight, and when he banged on the window, the surprise caused my bladder to leak. He asked for my license and proof of insurance and appeared ready to take his good old time. I handed them over, fighting the temptation to ask him to hurry up and write me a ticket. He asked if I knew why he had pulled me over. I didn't have time to play this game. I said, I know I was speeding. Can you please just hurry up and write me the ticket. I have to get out of here. He was holding a flashlight he had been shining down at my license he had placed on a clipboard. He clenched his jaw and shone the light in my eyes. The bright beam reflected off my seething anger, and I felt no impulse to look away.

He said, What exactly is the hurry?

Recently on a stretch of highway near where I was a trooper had pulled over a young college student who was speeding his dog to an emergency veterinary clinic. The encounter was caught on the trooper's dashboard-mounted video camera. While the driver pleaded with the trooper to let him get back on the road, the trooper took his time, telling the driver there were plenty of other dogs out there if his died. The dog did die. Sometimes I consider modifying my opposition to capital punishment where child and animal abusers are involved.

I said, Officer, I am a lawyer and I have an emergency. He waited for me to go on, skeptical there is such a thing as a legal emergency at nine o'clock at night in the middle of nowhere. I said, I am a death-penalty lawyer and there is an execution scheduled for right now.

He hadn't heard that one before. He lowered the clipboard and shone his light at the ground. He said, Prosecution or defense?

If you've never been tempted to lie, you've never been in love. Truthfulness is overrated. The world works the way we want it to because of a thousand little innocent lies. I suddenly realized that in the back of my mind I had started fashioning my story as soon as I saw his strobe. Any story would do. I had to get out of here. My phone rang. I said to the trooper, It's my office, and I answered. Still no news. He said, I asked whether you are prosecution or defense.

Fuck it. I was just so tired of this. I practically spit it out. I said, I represent the defendant.

He had started to glance down at his clipboard, but his head jerked up, like a fishing pole when the diving fish snaps the line. He had the heel of his right hand on the butt of his holstered gun. He bent forward from the waist so his face was framed in the window. I was not going to look away. He would have to blink.

I won. He broke the stare and stood upright and looked down at my license. I thought to myself, Shit. What have I done.

The trooper placed the clipboard under his arm and grasped the door frame with both his hands. He said, Sir, I have been in law enforcement for thirty years. I had a friend, a guard in Huntsville, who was killed when the Churrasco gang tried to break out. Do you remember that? He left a wife and three baby daughters. I still sit next to them in church every Sunday. I am a Christian, sir. I do not believe it is man's province to carry out God's punishment. Not all my fellow officers agree. I've always found it perplexing that God's word is truth, but His creatures disagree as to its meaning.

He tore my ticket in half and dropped the pieces on the passenger seat. He said, I'll radio up ahead so you don't have any more problems. Please do me a favor and keep it under a hundred.

■ ■ ■

THE WARDEN WAS WAITING for me when I got to the prison at ten minutes after ten. A guard started to pass a metal-detecting wand over me. The warden waved him away and said, Follow me. We walked back to the holding cell where I had visited with Ezekiel Green not two weeks before. It was nighttime, like the old days, when they carried out executions at midnight, and as we crossed the small patch of grass, I looked up and saw a sky full of stars. I saw Saturn and next to it Regulus, brightest star in Leo, Leo the Lion, king of the jungle, powerful and fearless, the opposite of me.

Sitting at the ocean's edge and staring out to sea, or lying in an open field and looking at the heavens, I experience the same feeling that might well be the opposite of awe. It is the powerful realization that nothing means anything. The universe is so big and so old, and we are so small and so ephemeral, that the very concept of our *place* in the world is an absurdity. None of my dichotomies makes any sense. Whether I am a good husband or a philanderer, a loving father or an absent one, a caring lawyer or an indifferent hack, is so trivial as to be irrelevant. *Trivial* is too big a word. They matter about as much as whether Winona chews up half a pair of Katya's expensive shoes or whether I smash a cockroach. You can laugh at your smallness or cry. The result's the same. Nobody cares whether Quaker lives or dies, and nobody should, because nothing is worth caring about.

Well, at least that's what I tried to tell myself.

The danger of perspective is that it can cause one to conclude that everything is just an aesthetic choice. Whether you are good or bad, assuming those words even mean anything, is, morally speaking, roughly equivalent to whether you prefer chocolate or vanilla. You can disbelieve that if you want. Like I said, belief is a choice. But truth has nothing to do with whether you believe it.

■ ■ ■

WHEN THE WARDEN SWUNG OPEN the heavy door and I saw Quaker in the holding cell, he was listening to an Al Green CD and—I am not making this up—dancing. The warden looked over at the three guards and furrowed his brow. They dropped their heads but made no move to unplug the music. The warden quietly closed the door behind me. I did not hear it lock. Quaker held up his right hand like a cop stopping traffic and sang a song about being tired of being alone. He asked one of the guards to turn it down a little and said to me, I love the reverend. Then, What's going on? Why's this taking so long?

I asked one of the guards if I could sit in the cell with Quaker. He said, This'll probably get me fired, then he swung open the door and I walked inside. I stuck out my hand. Quaker paused, still cautious and reserved, then smiled a huge smile and took my hand in both of his. He pulled me toward him, like I was a scared dog on a leash, which wasn't far from the truth, and when he let my hand go, I felt as awkward as a boy on a first date who doesn't know whether to kiss the girl. Quaker wrapped his arms around me, and I hugged him back. His eyes were moist, but—and this is the craziest thing—he seemed almost happy.

The phone rang and one of the guards answered it. Quaker said, It's peculiar, I know, but I feel really good. I know why they call it being at peace. I've been buzzing on the inside for so long, and now it's calm, like the ocean with no waves. Even this morning on the row, all this noise and banging, all the usual shit, but it was like muffled, like I was underwater or something.

The guard hung up the phone and told us it was time to go. Quaker smiled again and nodded at me. Shouldn't he have been shackled? Was he shackled? He said, I hope Pascal bet right. I want to see my Dorris, and my babies. But you know what? Even if I don't get to, I don't want to be here anymore without them. You know what I'm saying, Professor? Either way I win.

I said, It's been a privilege to represent you, Henry.

He said, Do me a favor and don't be second-guessing all your decisions for once. I know what you did for me. I know you believe me. Tell them lawyers in your office how much I appreciate it.

I will. I will.

And here. Please give this to my mama and tell her I love her.

He handed me his Bible. He hugged me again. He whispered in my ear, Thank you. I might have felt his lips brush against my cheek.

The guard who had answered the phone said, I think we got to go now, Henry.

The guard called Henry by his name. Funny that's what I remember.

■   ■   ■

Two of the guards took Henry by either arm. The third opened the door to the courtyard for me and pointed me toward the door for the witnesses. When the door closed behind me, I heard Henry singing.

My phone rang. Kassie told me what I had already inferred. She said, The Supremes denied us. It was five to four. The governor turned us down, too.

I felt my heart quicken. In the Supreme Court, there is something called the rule of four. With only a few exceptions, nobody has an automatic right to have the Supreme Court consider his appeal. You have to get permission. The legal device used to make this request is the petition for writ of certiorari. By a long-standing convention of the Court, if four justices want to hear the case, the Court will hear it. This rule of four can create an anomaly. When a death-row inmate is facing execution, it takes five justices to grant a stay of execution. So it is possible for four justices to want to hear the case, but unless a fifth justice votes to grant a stay, the inmate will be executed before the Court can consider his case, and if the execution goes forward, there will be no case to hear. In the esoteric language of the law, the case will be rendered moot by the death of the petitioner. Many years ago, Justice Lewis Powell would always provide the fifth vote for a stay if four of his colleagues wanted to hear a case, but since Powell's retirement, nobody does that. Over the past few years, there have been more than a dozen inmates executed even though four justices wanted to hear their case, because no fifth justice would provide the necessary additional vote for a stay.

But I remembered something. Fifteen years earlier, the Supreme Court had agreed to hear the appeal of a Texas death-row inmate, and after the Court announced that decision, a trial court scheduled the inmate's execution. The Texas Court of Criminal Appeals stepped in and granted the inmate a stay. According to the Texas court, if the Supreme Court had agreed to hear the case, then it would be unseemly for the State of Texas to carry out an execution in the interim. I said to Kassie, We have to file something in state court and ask for a stay so that the Supreme Court can consider the appeal. I told her of another case where we had made a similar argument, so she and the others could work off those pleadings as a template. I said, Call me as soon as it's filed.

Then I called the attorney general. Charles Allred was the assistant assigned to the case. I'd met him once. He looked barely old enough to shave. People who are so young that they still believe themselves to be immortal should be barred from facilitating death. I told him we intended to file something and explained our theory. I said, I know your usual practice is not to go forward with an execution while an appeal is pending, and I just want to make sure that you all will wait to go forward until our appeal is disposed of.

But nothing is pending yet, right?

It will be within the next few minutes.

It was ten fifty. He said, I'll give you until eleven, and he hung up.

After the fiasco surrounding the Buckley execution, when the court of appeals had closed before we could file our papers, that court instituted a system for electronic filings. Kassie called. She said, It's short, and it's not very good, but it's ready. Do you want to look at it? I told her just to file it and then to call Allred.

I said, Thanks for getting it done. Call me as soon as you hear something.

I had been standing in the courtyard, right beside the door that opened into the area for the inmate's witnesses. There were separate doors leading to other areas for witnesses related to the victim, and for the press. There were no witnesses for the victims, so both those rooms were being used for press. A reporter named Marcus Godbold walked outside and said to me, Aren't you going to come in? They're getting ready to start.

Are you sure?

Well, they just opened the curtain, and your guy's on the gurney.

■　■　■

ONCE ON THE LOWER Guadalupe River, a five-mile stretch of whitewater in central Texas that's mellow except when it's flooded, one of the kayakers in a group a quarter mile downriver from me missed his roll three times on the swollen river and had to swim. He got pinned between his boat and a massive tree. Water was pouring over his head. He was screaming, I don't want to drown, don't let me die. I was running the river with Craig. We both had throw ropes, and I had taken a swiftwater-rescue course, but that was pretend. My real-life experience with treacherous rescues was nil. Craig paddled into a two-boat eddy behind a boulder as big as a truck. I followed him in. He pointed to a spot on the bank, and said, Let's set up rescue lines there. It was so loud I wasn't sure I had heard him. I wasn't sure I wanted to hear him. He wedged his boat between two rocks and went scurrying toward the spot.

Two hours later, we were at the takeout, washing down Snickers bars with bottles of Fat Tire, which tastes a lot better than it sounds. I was glad Craig had been there. If it had been up to me, I might just have paddled on, hoping the guy would make it, leaving his rescue to his buddies and the EMTs. I would have read the papers and checked out the whitewater paddling Web sites, looking for news. It would have bothered me forever. I don't know anybody who wants to be paralyzed by panic.

Maybe I learned something from that experience. But like I said, lessons lose something in translation. When the reporter told me Henry was on the gurney, I had no idea what to do.

■　　■　　■

INMATES ARE EXECUTED by a cocktail of three chemicals. The first is a barbiturate that makes the inmate go to sleep. The second causes paralysis. The third induces cardiac arrest. They give the second drug for the sake of the witnesses. If the inmate were not paralyzed, he would flop around like a fish out of water when the third drug stopped his heart. The first drug is for the sake of the inmate. If he doesn't get enough of it, he will feel himself suffocating to death after his diaphragm is paralyzed from drug number two, and the third drug will inflict excruciating pain, like pouring muriatic acid into an open wound.

Two executioners sit in a separate room and watch for the warden's signal through a strip of one-way glass. The warden stands at the inmate's feet, next to a phone. He reads the death warrant out loud, and before he nods to get things under way, he calls the attorney general and the governor's office to make sure it's appropriate to proceed.

I called the office. Gary answered. I said, Get the goddamned thing filed.

It's almost done.

They've got Quaker on the gurney. Just file it.

He said, Hold on. I heard him shout to Kassie.

Impotence is unremarkable. Of the millions of Jews slaughtered in the Holocaust, some of them were children who died while their powerless parents watched. Hundreds of people a year get executed in China, Iran, Iraq, and Sudan, and the government bills the family for the cost of the bullet to the brain. I read about a woman who was watching her husband and their

244

two children climb a mountain in Austria. The daughter fell, their arrest lines snapped, and all three plunged to their deaths. Did she scream? Did she run toward them? I read about a man holding his twin boys on a roof in Haiti during a hurricane. One slipped and the raging flood waters carried him away. Did the man think about jumping in after him? Did he cover his other son's eyes?

Is there any shame in not going through meaningless motions? You can throw yourself into the gears, but most of the times jet engines suck in a bunch of birds, the plane keeps on flying.

I called Connie, the warden's assistant, and asked her how I could call the phone in the chamber. She said she didn't know. I did not believe her, but I didn't have time to argue. I called the one judge on the court of appeals whose cell number I know and got her voice mail. I called Allred's office and got his, too. Who else could I call? What could I do? I couldn't think. I couldn't move. I couldn't do a thing. I called Allred's boss. After the fourth ring, Marcus Godbold opened the door to the courtyard again. He said, You better hurry up.

■　　■　　■

I RAN INTO THE WITNESS ROOM. I said, I'm here, Henry, but I had no idea whether he could hear me. I heard him talking to the men who were next to him.

He was saying, I truly am innocent. One day, I hope somebody will prove that. Dorris was the love of my life. Daniel and

Charisse were our greatest joys. I could never have harmed them, and their deaths destroyed me. Not a single minute of a single day has gone by that I haven't missed them terribly. He looked at me. He said, And you believed me.

I could see a single tear spill out of each of his eyes. He looked at the two guards standing on either side of him. He looked into the room where the executioners were. He looked at the warden. He said, When the truth comes out, I do not want any of you to feel guilty for what is happening here tonight. I mean it sincerely. You all have treated me fairly and with respect. You've done what you had to do. I respect that. This is not your doing, or your fault, or in your control.

The warden squeezed the bridge of his nose. One of the guards wiped his eyes with his forearm. Henry looked at the warden. He said, That's it.

The warden seemed lost for a moment. Then he took a copy of the death warrant and read it out loud. He asked Henry if he had a statement. Henry said, Warden, I'm ready.

The newspaper the next day would say that Henry started softly to sing a Psalm. It wasn't a Psalm. I recognized it. It was a Tracy Chapman song. He was singing about saving a space in your heart. But who was he singing to? Dorris? The children? Was he saving the space, or was someone else supposed to save it for him? These are the questions I wanted to ask. He turned his head and faced the window separating him from me. Could he see through it, or was he seeing his reflection? I think I might have shaken my head. He smiled, like it was a joke. He had to be able to see me. He said, Thank you, man. Thank you. Then he faced the ceiling and sang again.

This could not be happening. We had an appeal pending. My head fell against the window, like a Muslim in prayer. The warden nodded at someone, and instantly a guard was behind me, his hand on my shoulder. I said to no one, We have an appeal still pending. Could anybody hear me?

He seemed to relax. I said, I'm here, Henry. I'm here. I'm standing right here.

He turned his head toward me. He mouthed, *Good-bye.* He coughed gently and closed his eyes.

No.

I slumped down onto the floor, my back against the wall separating me from him. I heard a chaplain repeating a monotonous prayer. I watched him play with his beads. I felt my phone vibrate in my pocket. I did not look down to see who it was.

At 11:37 p.m. the doctor pronounced him dead.

■　■　■

EARLIER I SAID life has no lessons. That's not exactly true. There are lessons, but only for the wise. If you don't learn them, you have only yourself to blame. There might not be anything you can do about it, but it's still your own fault. Fault and free will are unrelated ideas.

We represented a death-row inmate named Darrin Grand. The judge who presided over his trial had carried on an affair for more than ten years with the district attorney who prosecuted Grand. At the time, each was married to someone else. They kept their relationship secret.

People don't care about murderers, or about the constitutional rights of men like Darrin Grand, but right and wrong aren't a matter of popular sentiment. If you were getting a divorce, and you found out the judge was sleeping with your spouse's lawyer, how confident would you be that the judge was fair? Maybe you can't imagine getting a divorce. Do you want the pitcher's father calling balls and strikes when your kid is standing at the plate?

Two weeks before Grand was supposed to be executed, an assistant district attorney gave us an affidavit confirming that his boss had been sleeping with the judge. We filed an appeal citing the alleged affair. The court of appeals ruled against us, saying that all we had was rumor and statements from third parties. They demanded proof of the affair with firsthand evidence. The appellate court's theory boiled down to this: Since the trial judge and the DA weren't talking, the state could go ahead and execute Mr. Grand, even if everyone else in the courthouse, from the other judges all the way down to the nighttime cleanup crew, swore the affair had gone on.

Some days murderers steal my spirit. Most of the time, though, it's judges.

But for every ten or twenty gutless panderers, there's a soul that houses righteous indignation. One of them lived north of Dallas, and we won the lotto when our case was randomly assigned to his court. He ordered the former judge and prosecutor to sit for depositions. One of law's mysteries is the power of the oath. Witnesses swear to tell the truth, and they usually do. Even presidents can't resist. The DA and the trial judge both admitted to the affair.

But none of that happened until many months later, and it never would have happened at all if Grand hadn't managed to escape being executed on the night the court of appeals turned us down. After the state court denied our request for a stay at eight o'clock in the evening, we decided to file something else. We more or less made it up as we were writing it. It had no chance of succeeding. None. It was such a feeble theory that, as I write these words, I can't even remember what it was. All I know is that it was like heaving the ball toward the hoop after all the fans have left the arena, the lights have been dimmed, and the officials have taken the basket down.

Pursuit of futility, however, is not necessarily a futile pursuit. By the time the other side filed its response, and by the time the appellate court ruled against us yet again, it was half past eleven. Prison officials said they could not carry out the execution in the remaining half hour. They put Grand back in the van and returned him to death row.

We had run out the clock. We kept Grand alive for a little longer, and in that time we stole, we proved what the judges on the court of appeals probably thought—what they secretly hoped—we never would, which is why Grand is still alive today. There is no such thing as delay for the sake of delay, because delay's shadow is where relief often lurks.

Why hadn't I remembered Grand? Why hadn't I done something to stall? I could have kept banging on the window. I could have struggled with the guard if he tried to pull me away. I could have barged into the press witness area and shouted to

249

them what was going on. I could have tried to barricade myself in the holding cell. Maybe the guards would have cooperated. Nobody knows. I did not even try to stop them from escorting an innocent man to his death. I was a German watching the brownshirts take my neighbor. I could have rushed into the execution chamber. I could have caused a commotion. I could have tried. I did none of that. I stood there. I was idle. I was a man making phone calls, a wordsmith, a debater, an analyst.

I could have, I could have, I could have. The three words that enable all evil.

Quaker needed action. I gave him tears.

■　■　■

I CALLED THE OFFICE. Kassie put me on the speaker and I told them all what had happened. I could hear their silence. My brother Steven keeps telling me I need to hire a grief counselor. He should know. He also works with people who are staving off the flood with teaspoons. One committed suicide last year; she hanged herself in the basement, right next to the washer and dryer. I talked to them until I was sure they were as okay as one can be, and told them I'd see them tomorrow.

Katya was in bed watching TV. I said, I can tell you about it in the morning. Don't wait up for me.

I want to. Are you okay?

Not yet.

I returned phone calls from reporters at the *Houston Chron-*

icle, the *Dallas Morning News,* the *Austin American Statesman,* the *Chicago Tribune,* and the *New York Times.* I like all the reporters, but that's not the reason I called them back. I called them so I did not have to be alone with my thoughts.

■   ■   ■

Maybe he did do it. It's not impossible.

■   ■   ■

Jennifer Hecht wrote a book called *Doubt.* There's a thirteen-question quiz near the beginning (e.g., *Do you believe that some thinking being consciously made the universe?*; *Do you believe that the world is not completely knowable by science?*). According to Hecht's scoring scale, I am *a hard-core atheist... of a certain variety: a rationalist materialist.* I took offense at that. That's not me at all. I'm a deeply spiritual person.

I was tempted to go back over the quiz and change a few of my answers from *yes* to *not sure* so that my grade would accord with reality. But I couldn't bring myself to lie.

Doesn't that prove that I was right and she is wrong?

Maybe belief isn't a choice after all. Maybe truth is.

■   ■   ■

I GOT HOME at a little after two. Winona was waiting for me in the kitchen and followed me up the stairs. Lincoln was sleeping on our bed. Katya was reading. She said, He asked if he could sleep in here so we could all be together.

I sat down next to her. I rested my head on her shoulder and stifled a sob and told her all of it. Lincoln woke up. He said, Hi, Dada. What time is it?

I said, It's late, amigo. Go back to sleep.

Okay. Good night.

Katya and I held hands and watched him. I ran my fingers through her hair. Neither of us said anything. There wasn't anything to say.

When I got out of the shower, Katya had fallen asleep with the book on her chest. Winona's legs were twitching, her head on Lincoln's hip. I poured brandy into a snifter and sat in the rocking chair at the foot of the bed. I picked up a book of Anne Carson poems. *Anger is a bitter lock*, she says. *But you can turn it.*

I turned off the lamp and closed the book. I sat there rocking, watching them sleep, hearing them breathe, my pillars.

AFTERWORD

Early the next morning, two hours before dawn, I got dressed in the dark and walked quietly downstairs. I swallowed four aspirins with a quart of water and left a note for Katya on the kitchen counter. I clipped a flashing reflector to my backpack, got on my bike, and headed back to work. We had another client set for execution the following week, and we had a lot to do.

At my office I couldn't find the coffee. Usually by the time I arrive somebody's already made it. It bothered me that I wasn't sure who. I rode the elevator back downstairs and crossed the street to the coffee shop. There were workers inside, but the doors were still locked. I sat on a bench outside and waited. I watched two trains pass, a northbound crossing Buffalo Bayou toward the University of Houston, and one heading south to the medical center. Both were packed full of commuters. I could see their blank faces under the fluorescent glare. It was too light to see any stars, but there was Venus, sitting right beside the pockmarked crescent moon, winking at me from low in the western sky.

Henry Quaker had been dead almost six hours.

I bought a large americano with an extra shot and a navel orange. Back in front of my computer, I sipped the coffee as I read through yesterday's e-mail, mostly condolences and a bit of spam. A couple were from people telling me he got what he deserved. I wrote them back and said, Thanks for your thoughtful note.

The weekend before the presidential election, my wife, brother, and I walked door-to-door in rural western Missouri canvassing for Obama. We bought sandwiches at a luncheonette where a skinny white guy squinted at our Obama buttons and whispered, I'm voting for him. Later we rang the bell at a dilapidated A-frame house set back far from a rutted dirt road. Three mangy dogs were chained out front to massive pines. A young pregnant woman holding a baby on her hip said she would never vote for someone who wouldn't even put his hand on the Bible. Katya wanted to explain to her that she was confused, that Obama is a Christian. I whispered, Let's go back to the car. People who form firm opinions with so little knowledge only pretend to be open-minded. They select their facts like food from a buffet.

In *Executed on a Technicality*, the book of mine Ezekiel Green said he read, my objective was to educate people about how the death penalty works. One reviewer said the book was about my cases, but not at all about me. She was exactly right. Maybe it was a mistake to write it that way, but it wasn't accidental. I wanted to write about facts. My beliefs were irrelevant.

But it is your beliefs, not just facts, that determine who you are. Of the hundred or more death-row inmates I've represented, there are seven, including Quaker, I believe to be innocent. They get sentenced to death because they have incompetent or underpaid trial lawyers, and because human beings make mistakes. They get executed because my colleagues and I can't find a way to stop it. Quaker won't be the last. I tell young lawyers who want to be death-penalty lawyers that if it's going to be disabling to watch your clients die, you need to find something else to do. Your clients are going to die. And it's not a comfort to know that most of them are guilty. The inmate set to die the week after the Quaker execution had murdered a woman and raped her, in that order. But if you believe it's wrong to kill, you believe it's wrong to kill. When I first met him, he said to me, All praise be to Allah for sending me here. I was on the wrong path, and until I got here I didn't know it. He believed he would not be executed. He thought it mattered that he had reformed. His older brother was a marine. He told me if he got paroled he wanted to go to Iraq and fight for his country.

Quaker and Winston and Green and all the rest are not their real names, but their cases are real. The courts and judges behaved in the manner I have described. I think some judges should be removed from the bench, but I don't think Judge Truesdale did anything legally unethical, or I would have said so. I haven't held much back. She cared about doing the right thing in the Quaker case. Lots of things are legal and also wrong.

As I was finishing this book, Katya, Lincoln, the dog, and I were in Park City, Utah. There were no executions scheduled in Texas for another month. We were hiking along Yellow Pine creek, up in the Uinta mountains, a few miles north of Kamas. We wanted to hike through the forest up to the lake, but three miles in, Lincoln said he was tired and asked if we could turn around. We said okay, and Lincoln took off sprinting, back toward the trailhead, the dog on his heels. We stopped to watch them.

I began talking to Katya about the book. I told her I felt like it was missing something, but I wasn't sure what. I said, The book is as factually truthful as I am allowed to be, and as emotionally honest as I am capable of being.

Katya said, Without years of therapy, anyway.

I smiled. We walked on along the creek, craning to keep Lincoln in sight.

The cases I have written about are not unusual. My other cases, every death-penalty lawyer's cases, are just like them. What's missing is the proof that what you have just finished reading is mundane. The day after Henry Quaker got put to death, my colleagues and I went back to the office and did it all over again, and all the same things happened.

I realized what's missing: all the other cases.

Lincoln waited for us to catch up at the edge of a pasture. A couple dozen cows were grazing and lowing loudly. The moms hustled to get between their young calves and us. Katya's afraid of cows. She walked closer to me. Lincoln said, Mama, maybe you should get a baby cow and that way when it grows up you won't be scared.

Lincoln and the dog ran ahead again. When we caught up to them, Lincoln was sitting on the ground, leaning against an aspen, and the dog was drinking from the creek. Dark clouds were forming in the west. The setting sun sank behind them and streaked the sky with wisps of purple and orange. The wind blew down from the north, and the air held a hint of chill. Lincoln asked whether we could make a fire when we got home.

AFTERWORD

In a couple of days, or maybe in a week, I'd have to start working on the next execution. But at that moment, as we walked slowly back toward where we had started, the three of us with the dog, all we talked about was what we would fix for dinner that night, and when we would come back to this spot, and about where we would go tomorrow.

ACKNOWLEDGMENTS

I hear there are solo practitioners. But for me, the practice of law has always been a collaborative enterprise. Andrea Keilen is the supremely talented executive director of the Texas Defender Service. I thank her and the actual TDS lawyers with whom I work every day, including on all the cases described in this book: Kate Black, Frances Bourliot, Matt Byrne, Kathryn Kase, Alma Lagarda, John Niland, Katherine Scardino, Jared Tyler, and Greg Wiercioch. (Gloria Flores, Nick Mensch, Melissa Waters, Rindy Fox, Ariell Hardy, Neil Hartley, Kelly Josh, Susanna Trevino, and Jessica Lindley, while nonlawyers, help keep the place running.) Steve Hall and Laura Burstein are also routinely helpful, and George Kendall's advice is routinely indispensable. The TDS interns are passionate and tireless.

Then there are the past (or almost) TDS lawyers who also worked on the cases described here, including: Melissa Azadeh, Sandra Babcock, Bryce Benjet, Dick Burr, Nicole Casarez, Mike Charlton, Phyllis Crocker, Karen Dennison, Mia de Saint Victor, Mike Gross, Andrew Hammel, Keith Hampton, Eden Harrington, Scott Howe, Cassandra Jeu, Lynn Lamberty, Maurie Levin, Jim Marcus, Joe Margulies, Robert McGlasson, Morris Moon, Brent Newton, Rob Owen, Jeff Pokorak, Danalynn Recer, Meredith Rountree, Raoul Schoneman, Naomi Terr, Jean

ACKNOWLEDGMENTS

Terranova, Mandy Welch, and Phil Wischkaemper. I've also been privileged to work with Tony Amsterdam, John Blume, Steve Bright, John Holdridge, Lee Kovarski, Greg Kuykendall, Paul Mansur, Nina Morrison, Barry Scheck, Jordan Steiker, Clive Stafford-Smith, Brian Stull, and Christina Swarns. I'm sure I've forgotten several people. I hope they'll forgive me.

I am grateful to Eric Holz, the surgeon who saved my eye. I owe an enormous debt as well to my friends Bowes Hamill and Charles Katz, gifted physicians who never asked me to stop calling or e-mailing, even though I called or e-mailed so often that I almost caused myself embarrassment.

Dean Ray Nimmer, Associate Dean Richard Alderman, and former dean Nancy Rapoport have supported my work at every step of the way, no matter how strong the headwinds—and they can indeed be strong. My students, both at the University of Houston Law Center and Rice University, have been indispensable and inspirational.

For reading the manuscript or discussing sensitive issues about it with me, I am grateful to many people, including: my brother Mark Dow, the best reader and writer I know; Marcilynn Burke, Seth Chandler, Meredith Duncan, Michael Olivas, and Ron Turner, extraordinary colleagues and even better friends; my friend David Jones, whose convoluted analyses are usually worth untangling; Simon Lipskar, my dedicated agent, whose advice and judgment are invariably spot-on; also at Writers House, Maja Nikolic, Angharad Kowal, and Jennifer Kelaher, who tirelessly promoted this book, and Josh Getzler, who exhibited immense patience in dealing with me; Jonathan Karp, the remarkable editor and publisher who intuitively understood

ACKNOWLEDGMENTS

exactly what I wanted to do with this book and who turned a manuscript I liked into a book I like much more, and his terrific assistant, Colin Shepherd, who was calming and resourceful; and finally, my dear friend Jon Liebman, whose faithfulness, wisdom, and friendship I've been benefiting from for longer than I care to say.

Katya and Lincoln held veto power over the book. That I've written it reflects that they said I could. They've allowed me to steal, shape, and share our stories. They've also allowed me to steal my way into their lives. I'm a lucky guy.

APPENDIX

Ethics Opinion for *The Autobiography of an Execution*

Meredith J. Duncan

Publisher's Note: In light of recent controversies regarding the authenticity of memoirs, we asked a professor of law specializing in legal ethics to explain the rules that constrain a lawyer's freedom to disclose privileged and confidential information. Her essay follows. While recognizing that some readers prefer documented sources in a work of nonfiction, David R. Dow made the decision to disguise identities of some characters to comply with ethical rules mandated by his profession.

Lawyers are ethically obligated to keep their clients' secrets, often forever. This obligation, which places serious limitations on an attorney's ability to write about his experiences, stems from two different bodies of law—evidence law, which defines the attorney-client privilege, and the legal ethics rules, which provide the contours of a lawyer's duty of confidentiality.[1]

The evidentiary attorney-client privilege protects communication between an attorney and the client from being revealed

---

[1] *See* MODEL RULES OF PROF'L CONDUCT R. 1.6 (2008) cmt. [3] (explaining distinction between attorney-client privilege and duty of confidentiality). Throughout this piece, I will often refer to the American Bar Association's MODEL RULES OF PROFESSIONAL CONDUCT. Although ethical standards vary from jurisdiction to jurisdiction, the MODEL RULES have been quite influential, having been adopted in large part by the majority of jurisdictions.

in court or other official proceeding.[2] When a client communicates with a lawyer seeking legal advice, that communication is protected by the evidentiary privilege. Consequently, the lawyer cannot be compelled to reveal that communication unless the client consents (or another limited exception applies).[3]

A lawyer's ethical duty of confidentiality is much broader than the evidentiary privilege.[4] This legal norm prohibits lawyers from discussing their clients' affairs. This duty of confiden-

---

[2] The attorney-client privilege is one of the oldest privileges recognized in common law. In its classic form, it provides that confidential communication between an attorney and client is protected from disclosure forever unless waived. *See* 8 J. WIGMORE, EVIDENCE, § 2292 (McNaughton rev. 1961). Based on this classic formulation, all modern jurisdictions recognize the attorney-client privilege. *See, e.g.,* FED. R. EVID. 501 (providing that attorney-client privilege "shall be governed by the principles of the common law as they may be interpreted by the courts of the United States in light of reason and experience"); CAL. EVID. CODE § 954 (2003) (providing that "the client, whether or not a party, has a privilege to refuse to disclose, and to prevent another from disclosing, a confidential communication between client and lawyer"); TEX. R. EVID. 503 (providing that a "client has a privilege to refuse to disclose and to prevent any other person from disclosing confidential communications made for the purpose of facilitating the rendition of professional legal services to the client").

[3] Commonly recognized exceptions to the attorney-client privilege are usually limited to the crime-fraud exception (when the client consults with the attorney for the purpose of committing a future crime or fraud) and the testamentary exception (where a testator's communication with counsel in drafting a will is revealed in order to establish testamentary intent). *See Swidler & Berlin v. United States*, 524 U.S. 399, 409–10 (1998) (discussing these limited exceptions to the attorney-client privilege).

[4] *See* MODEL RULES OF PROF'L CONDUCT R. 1.6(a) (2008) (providing that a "lawyer shall not reveal information relating to the representation of a client unless the client gives informed consent").

tiality protects all information relating to the representation of the client, regardless of its source.[5] It prohibits an attorney from revealing *any* information about a client, in or outside of a courtroom, whether known to others or not, and regardless of whether the lawyer learned the information from the client or someone else. This ethical obligation means that a lawyer may not reveal information relating to a client's matter to others unless the client agrees to its disclosure (or one of a few limited exceptions applies).[6] It is primarily his duty of confidentiality that is at stake when a lawyer decides to pen a memoir.

Both the attorney-client privilege and the duty of confidentiality are driven by two essential considerations: (1) promoting candor and honesty within the attorney-client relationship[7] and (2) maintaining an appearance of loyalty.[8] When clients speak to their lawyers, it is desirable for clients to be as open and honest with counsel

[5] *See* MODEL RULES OF PROF'L CONDUCT R. 1.6 cmt. [3] (2008) ("The confidentiality rule...applies not only to matters communicated in confidence by the client but also to all information relating to the representation, whatever its source").

[6] *See* MODEL RULES OF PROF'L CONDUCT R. 1.6(b) (2008) (setting forth exceptions to the duty of confidentiality, which include preventing reasonably certain death or substantial bodily harm or preventing client from committing a financial crime or fraud).

[7] *See Swidler & Berlin*, 524 U.S. at 403 ("The privilege is intended to encourage 'full and frank communication between attorneys and their clients and thereby promote broader public interests in the observance of law and the administration of justice'" [quoting *Upjohn Co. v. United States*, 449 U.S. 383 (1981)]); MODEL RULES OF PROF'L CONDUCT R. 1.6 cmt. [2] (2008) (explaining that ethical duty of confidentiality encourages clients to speak "fully and frankly" with their lawyers, "even as to embarrassing or legally damaging subject matter").

[8] *See* MODEL RULES OF PROF'L CONDUCT R. 1.6 cmt. [2] (2008) (describing trust as "hallmark" of attorney-client relationship).

as possible, and these rules further that degree of openness. Good legal representation is facilitated by the lawyer's knowing every-thing that the client knows, even if those things may be embarras-ing or could be potentially harmful to the client or others.[9] In an effort to ensure that a client feels safe in disclosing all the lawyer may need to know, the law protects virtually all the communication between the lawyer and the client (as long as the communication occurred in the context of the attorney-client relationship).

In some circumstances, the privilege or duty of confidentiality may yield and permit the attorney to reveal otherwise confidential information. So, for example, when revealing confidential infor-mation may prevent the client from committing a future crime, an attorney is permitted to reveal that information.[10] Similarly, when the attorney's revelation of confidential information may prevent reasonably certain death or bodily harm to another, the attorney is permitted to reveal confidential information.[11] The most recently recognized exceptions to the duty of confidential-ity allow for disclosure of confidential information in order to prevent a client from committing a financial or economic fraud.[12]

---

[9] See *Upjohn Co.*, 449 U.S. at 390–91 (explaining importance of attorney-client privilege in enabling attorney to know all facts that client knows in order to determine what is legally relevant [citing MODEL CODE PROF'L RESPONSIBIL-ITY EC 4-1 (1983)]).

[10] See, e.g., *United States v. Zolin*, 491 U.S. 554, 562–63 (1989) (describing pur-pose of crime-fraud exception to attorney-client privilege as preventing cli-ent from communicating with lawyer for purpose of obtaining advice for commission of future crime or fraud).

[11] See MODEL RULES OF PROF'L CONDUCT R. 1.6(b)(1) (2008).

[12] See MODEL RULES OF PROF'L CONDUCT R. 1.6(b)(2) & (3) (2008) (adopted in August 2003).

These exceptions have only recently been enacted, in response to the Enron scandal and other corporate abuses in which it was suspected that attorneys' revelation of confidential information might have prevented vast financial ruin to thousands of people, had the revelation been allowed.

The ethical rules constraining lawyers rest on the belief that frank conversation between a lawyer and clients is aided when clients can be confident that the conversations they have with their lawyers will never be used to embarrass or injure them.[13] Therefore, we assure clients that all communication with their lawyers relating to legal representation will be kept secret forever, unless they consent to disclosure. If a client dies without consenting to the disclosure of confidential information, a lawyer is bound to keep that information secret forever.[14]

An additional concern driving confidentiality rules is based on principles of agency law.[15] A lawyer is the client's agent. She stands as one with her client, helping the client navigate through the complexities of the legal system. The lawyer is to be her client's advocate and counselor, single-mindedly devoted to her client. Talking to others unnecessarily about her client's

---

[13] *See Swidler & Berlin*, 524 U.S. at 407 (explaining that clients concerned about reputation, civil liability, or possible harm to friends or family are more willing to be frank with their attorneys because of the attorney-client privilege).

[14] *See id.* at 410 ("It has been generally, if not universally, accepted...that the attorney-client privilege survives the death of the client").

[15] *See* MODEL RULES OF PROF'L CONDUCT R. 1.6 cmt. [2] (2008) (describing duty of confidentiality as contributing "to the trust that is the hallmark of the client-lawyer relationship").

affairs evokes images of disloyalty. To keep secrets inviolate indefinitely is to be at one with the client, to show the utmost loyalty, whether to a current or former client. The ethical obligation to maintain client confidences concerns this appearance of loyalty, as do other ethics rules, such as the rules governing conflicts of interest.[16] Keeping a client's secrets until told to do otherwise is part of being loyal, even if keeping the secrets means exhibiting that loyalty beyond the client's grave.[17]

Not being able to talk to family or friends, not even to a spouse, about a large part of one's life—the details of one's workdays—can exact a heavy toll on lawyers. Perhaps keeping clients' secrets—particularly where the stakes are very high or the secrets are dark—helps explain the high incidence of depression, substance abuse, and suicide within the legal community, one of the highest rates among those of all professions.[18]

Consider the recent story of attorneys Dale Coventry and Jamie Kunz. More than twenty-five years ago, Coventry and Kunz, Cook

---

[16] *See, e.g.,* MODEL RULES OF PROF'L CONDUCT R. 1.7 (governing concurrent conflicts of interest) & 1.9 (governing successive conflicts of interest).

[17] *See Swidler & Berlin*, 524 U.S. at 408 (recognizing potential loss of evidence due to privilege, but justifying the loss by explaining that without privilege, "the client may not have made such communications in the first place" so the "loss of evidence is more apparent than real").

[18] *See generally* Laura Rothstein, *Law Students and Lawyers with Mental Health and Substance Abuse Problems: Protecting the Public and Individual,* 69 U. PITT. L. REV. 531 (2008) (explaining that rates of depression and substance abuse are much higher than those of general population); Patrick J. Schiltz, *On Being a Happy, Healthy, and Ethical Member of an Unhappy, Unhealthy, and Unethical Profession,* 52 VAND. L. REV. 871 (1999) (discussing high rate of depression, mental health issues, and substance abuse within legal profession).

County public defenders, were assigned to represent Andrew Wilson against murder charges.[19] During that representation, Wilson confessed to his lawyers that he had robbed and murdered a security guard at a McDonald's restaurant in January 1982, a crime for which another man, Alton Logan, was being charged. Bound by the attorney-client privilege, Coventry and Kunz kept silent as Logan was ultimately convicted and sentenced to life in prison for a murder he did not commit. Andrew Wilson had given his attorneys permission to disclose his secret only upon the event of Wilson's death. In anticipation of that moment, in 1982, Coventry and Kunz executed an affidavit attesting to Wilson's admission. They kept the affidavit in a lock box under the bed in one of the men's bedrooms for a quarter of a century while Logan served prison time for a crime he did not commit. It was only in 2007, upon Wilson's death, that they produced the affidavit to the authorities. In 2008, Logan was released from prison.[20] Both Coventry and Kunz now speak openly about the angst and torment they suffered as a result of being ethically bound to keep Wilson's secret.[21] They also give thanks to their client, Wilson, for agreeing to allow them to disclose the secret, because without Wilson's permission, they would both have had to take that secret to their graves. Both Coventry and Kunz have been celebrated by the legal community for the ability to keep their

---

[19] *See* Maurice Possley, *Inmate's Freedom May Hinge on Secret Kept for 26 Years,* CHI. TRIB., Jan. 19, 2008.

[20] *See* Matthew Walberg, *South Side Man Finally Free After 26 Years,* CHI. TRIB., Sept. 5, 2008.

[21] *See* Possley, *supra* note 19 (describing how Wilson's attorneys were "haunted" over the years for not being able to disclose Wilson's confession).

client's secret.[22] In addition to being lauded by the legal community for keeping quiet for all these years, they should also be commended for having the foresight to acquire their client's permission to reveal his secret after his death. Coventry and Kunz have been much less well received by the community at large.[23]

Everyone loves a good story, and lawyer stories can be among the best. However, lawyers are prohibited from telling the very best ones—the ones about their real, everyday life experiences with their clients (a fact I must remind lawyers who visit my classroom of all the time). Lawyer "war stories" can be fascinating and entertaining, but without client consent, telling war stories is a violation of a lawyer's ethical obligations. A lawyer may discuss his cases only if there is no reasonable likelihood that the listener will be able to identify the actual client or case. Even a lawyer's "hypothetical" story is prohibited by the ethics rules if it could reasonably lead to the discovery of a client's identity, information, or the situation involved.[24] Similarly, labeling a story a work of fiction does not abrogate a lawyer's ethical obligation not to reveal client confidences.

---

[22] From a legal ethics position, their decision was not debatable. They had no option but to keep this secret, as it concerned a past crime. *See, e.g., United States v. Zolin*, 491 U.S. at 562–63 (explaining that attorney-client privilege protects communications regarding past crimes).

[23] *See, e.g., 60 Minutes* (CBS television broadcast Mar. 9, 2008) (covering story of Alton Logan and representation of Andrew Wilson by attorneys Dale Coventry and Jamie Kunz).

[24] *See* MODEL RULES OF PROF'L CONDUCT R. 1.6 cmt. [4] (2008) (providing that "lawyer's use of a hypothetical to discuss issues relating to the representation is permissible so long as there is no reasonable likelihood that the listener will be able to ascertain the identity of the client or the situation involved").

APPENDIX

At the outset of *The Autobiography of an Execution*, the author tells us that he has gone to great lengths to disguise particular identities in order to fulfill his ethical obligations. He is required to do so. His ability to provide the very best legal representation for his clients is dependent, in large part, on his clients' having confidence that their lawyer will keep their secrets forever. Even a lawyer who believes that it would benefit society to learn about the details of one of his cases, or who believes that it would be personally therapeutic to discuss one of his cases, confronts head-on the lawyer's obligation to keep secrets. Of course, the safest ethical choice is to remain silent. However, if the decision is to tell his story, the lawyer must be very careful not to reveal his client's identity, information, or confidences.

Meredith J. Duncan is the George Butler Research Professor of Law at the University of Houston Law Center, where she teaches in the areas of professional responsibility, legal ethics, criminal law, sexual assault law, and torts.

ABOUT THE AUTHOR

DAVID R. Dow is the University Distinguished Professor at the University of Houston Law Center, and the litigation director at the Texas Defender Service, a nonprofit legal aid corporation that represents death-row inmates. As an appellate lawyer, he has represented more than one hundred death-row inmates over the past twenty years. A graduate of Rice and Yale, Dow is the editor (with Mark Dow) of *Machinery of Death*, and the author of *Executed on a Technicality: Lethal Injustice on America's Death Row* and *America's Prophets: How Judicial Activism Makes America Great*, as well as a treatise on contract law. Dow is also the author of more than one hundred professional articles and essays, and his work has appeared in many popular publications, including the *New York Times*, the *Washington Post*, the *Christian Science Monitor*, the *Progressive*, the *Texas Observer*, the *Dallas Morning News*, and the *Houston Chronicle*. He resides with his wife, their son, and their dog in Houston.

ABOUT TWELVE

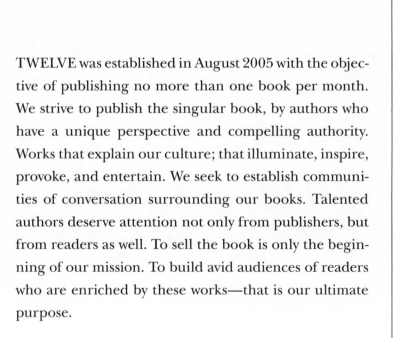

TWELVE

TWELVE was established in August 2005 with the objective of publishing no more than one book per month. We strive to publish the singular book, by authors who have a unique perspective and compelling authority. Works that explain our culture; that illuminate, inspire, provoke, and entertain. We seek to establish communities of conversation surrounding our books. Talented authors deserve attention not only from publishers, but from readers as well. To sell the book is only the beginning of our mission. To build avid audiences of readers who are enriched by these works—that is our ultimate purpose.